מסורה

The ArtScroll Series®

Rabbi Nosson Scherman / Rabbi Meir Zlotowitz

General Editors

There Will Never

by
Roiza D. Weinreich

Be Another You!

DEVELOPING A CUSTOMIZED PLAN TO REACH YOUR POTENTIAL

Published by

Mesorah Publications, ltd

FIRST EDITION
First Impression . . . December 1992

Published and Distributed by
MESORAH PUBLICATIONS, Ltd.
Brooklyn, New York 11232

Distributed in Israel by
MESORAH MAFITZIM / J. GROSSMAN
Rechov Harav Uziel 117
Jerusalem, Israel

Distributed in Australia & New Zealand by
GOLD'S BOOK & GIFT CO.
36 William Street
Balaclava 3183, Vic., Australia

Distributed in Europe by
J. LEHMANN HEBREW BOOKSELLERS
20 Cambridge Terrace
Gateshead, Tyne and Wear
England NE8 1RP

Distributed in South Africa by
KOLLEL BOOKSHOP
22 Muller Street
Yeoville 2198, Johannesburg
South Africa

THE ARTSCROLL SERIES®
THERE WILL NEVER BE ANOTHER YOU
© Copyright 1992, by MESORAH PUBLICATIONS, Ltd. and Mrs. Roiza D. Weinreich
4401 Second Avenue / Brooklyn, N.Y. 11232 / (718) 921-9000

No part of this book may be reproduced
in any form without **written** permission from the copyright holder,
except by a reviewer who wishes to quote brief passages in connection with a review
written for inclusion in magazines or newspapers.

THE RIGHTS OF THE COPYRIGHT HOLDER WILL BE STRICTLY ENFORCED.

ISBN:
0-89906-427-2 (hard cover)
0-89906-428-0 (paperback)

Printed in the United States of America by Noble Book Press Corp.
Bound by Sefercraft Quality Bookbinders, Ltd., Brooklyn, N.Y.

לזכר נשמת

In memory of my beloved grandparents

ר׳ נפתלי בנימין בן ר׳ משה

וזוגתו

האשה חוה בת ר׳ שאול

ר׳ משה בן ר׳ ברוך הכהן

וזוגתו

האשה מחלה בת ר׳ צבי יהודה

תנצב״ה

Acknowledgements

I would like to thank the many people who provided ideas and support during the process of writing this book.

Special thanks to Rabbi Avrohom Blumenkranz *Shlita* and Rabbi Ezriel Tauber *Shlita* for reviewing the manuscript, and for giving valuable guidance. Rabbi Abraham J. Twerski *Shlita* took out time from his busy schedule to respond promptly in a helpful and reassuring manner. My appreciation goes to Sara Lea Seltzer, Chaia Erblich, Esther Press, Miriam Kaufman, Georgie Klein, Yiska Gross, Manya Fisher, Goldie Miller, Laurie Corlin, Raizel Rivka Herbst, and Naomi Levin for contributing carefully thought out ideas and suggestions.

In Shalheves I have learned many of the book's themes, particularly at Rabbi Tauber's lectures, and presented many of its concepts as a steady speaker. Special thanks to Mrs. Gottlieb, Shalheves' administrator. My students at the Tuesday *Tehillim* class and the subscribers to my newsletter contributed most of the examples in the book. Henya Novick, Sara Lea Matkoff, Barbara Kesler and Malkie Treitel read the first draft and gave valuable recommendations. Faigy Silverman was thorough yet gentle with editing, and made important creative contributions. Our friendship has grown over the months that we worked together.

Gratitude goes to Rabbis Meir Zlotowitz and Nosson Scherman for putting their faith in this project and for their patience, and encouragement. My special thanks to Rabbi Sheah Brander whose expert knowledge made the book complete. Rabbi Avi Gold contributed substantially as well. Kudos to Rabbi Moshe Lieber, Mrs. Faygie Weinbaum, Mrs. Ethel Gottlieb, Mrs. Bassie Gutman,

Nichie Fendrich and Mindy Kohn of the ArtScroll staff. I consider it a privilege to participate in the ArtScroll Series.

My parents, Mr. and Mrs. Moshe Perlman and my mother-in-law, Mrs. Pearl Weinreich, have encouraged and sustained all my various undertakings. I hope they will always have *nachas* from all their children and grandchildren. When I first dreamed of writing, my husband Faivel brought a computer home. From that beginning he has been a constant source of encouragement and support.

The foundation of this book was the real life example of my father-in law — Harav Sholom ben Shraga Baruch, *zichrono levrachah*. Each hour of his life overflowed with energy, optimism, kindness to others and determination to serve Hashem and help Torah causes. Many who have suffered in life express dissatisfaction and resentment but his attitude was different. As a Holocaust survivor, his credo was, "Life is so precious. Let's not waste it on grumbling and griping ; let's enjoy and give joy during every moment."

וִיהִי נֹעַם ה׳ אֱלֹקֵינוּ עָלֵינוּ וּמַעֲשֵׂה יָדֵינוּ כּוֹנְנָה עָלֵינוּ וּמַעֲשֵׂה יָדֵינוּ כּוֹנְנֵהוּ,
May Hashem's Presence and Satisfaction rest upon us. May Hashem complete our efforts and assure their success. May the work of our hands establish Hashem's Kingdom on earth (Tehillim 90:17).

Foreword

by Abraham J. Twerski, MD

The past few years have produced a bumper crop of self-help books, focusing on the need for improving one's function and eliminating the various barriers that prevent full self-realization. The author is quite correct in her statement in the introduction that people who read these books often relapse into their usual methods of coping (or more correctly, perhaps, non-coping), and all the negative traits one sought to eliminate creep back in.

One of the reasons for this may be that the lack of self-confidence that is at the root of one's personality problems also operates to preclude taking corrective measures. Furthermore, the effort required to bring about change in oneself may be considerable, and one's inertia (or simply laziness) pulls one back to well-ingrained habits.

In this book the author makes several important contributions to enhance self-improvement. (1) She draws upon the authority of Torah writings that attest to our unrecognized and untapped personal resources; (2) she gives specific, concrete examples of how one can apply techniques to overcome negativity, and also provides exercises to follow; (3) she indicates that inasmuch as Torah requires that one maximize one's potential, a person is not at liberty to refrain from doing so for whatever reason, just as one may not rationalize why not to perform any other Torah requirement.

To the person already familiar or becoming familiar with Torah in its comprehensive sense, this book can show the way to a more efficient and happier life.

Table of Contents

Introduction: Recipes from Life 13
   Chart: My Goals in This Workshop 17
   Directions 18

Part I: Focusing On the Positive

Chapter 1
   Appreciating the "Little Things" 22
Chapter 2
   Appreciating Yourself 28
Chapter 3
   Appreciating Others 40
      Part 1: Defusing Interpersonal Tension 44
      Part 2: Breaking the Ice 49

Part II: Overcoming Obstacles

Chapter 4
   The Opportunities We Miss 58
Chapter 5
   Dispelling The Myths 68
Chapter 6
   Recovering From Past Failures 76
Chapter 7
   When Things Go Wrong 86
Chapter 8
   Anxiety About the Future: The Un-panic Button 94

Chapter 9
    The Impossible Dream   102

Chapter 10
    The Motivation To Grow   112

Part III: Wrapping Up

Chapter 11
    Preparing For the Future   126

Chapter 12
    A Daily Menu   134

Chapter 13
    The Last Word   142

Appendix
    Confidence In Public Speaking   145

Index   155

There Will Never Be Another You!

There has never been anyone exactly like you, and there will never be another you until the end of time.

Every person must remember: "I am a distinct individual with a precise combination of talents. I was born to these parents at this interval in history and in this particular place. Certainly G-d assigned a specific task to me. I have a special portion in Torah. The entire world is waiting for me. No other person in the world can accomplish my mission in life."

(Harav Shlomo Wolbe, *Alei Shur*)

Introduction

Have you ever resolved to begin a new project and then found that you could not carry it through?

Have you ever wasted an opportunity because you decided it would be better not to try than to fail?

Do you ever feel inadequate for any reason?

Have you ever compared yourself to someone else and felt that in a million years you could never be so accomplished?

Believe it or not, you are not alone. Many people set goals for themselves but somehow cannot find the tools to achieve them. Many people have visions of others which are so ideal that they feel small by comparison.

For me, the person I always wanted to emulate was my mother. When I was little, I thought she could do anything and I still think so. My parents owned a large machine shop that sold goods worldwide, and my mother was involved in every detail of the business. She walked several miles each day, touring the shop from one end to the other and supervising the workers.

She never felt, however, that her long hours at work excused shortcuts in the most important place of all — her home. She never cooked for *Shabbos* ahead of time because *Shabbos* food had to be fresh. She would get up at five A.M. on Friday morning and make the fish and desserts while I slept, and then she would rush home after work and put together the soup, *cholent*, and roast in a space of two hours.

My mother always worked in the shop until the day before *Pesach*, and yet she saw no problem in having twelve guests for the *Seder*. She could sew skillfully as well; after a long day at work she would often come home and add beautifully embroidered trimmings to my dresses.

When I grew older, I still saw my mother as a person who could cope with anything and keep smiling. I will never forget the wonderful occasion several years ago when, on a single afternoon, I watched her create several huge batches of *kreplach*, ice nut cakes, and decorate cookies for a family *simchah* — after she hadn't touched the mixer in sixteen years!

That episode reminded me of the first *Shabbos* meal I ever cooked in my own home. I worked diligently for this special occasion, but despite my efforts the soup tasted bland, and the *cholent* was watery and cold because I had not adjusted the fire properly. The only thing that turned out well was the fish which my mother had sent us.

How in the world did she manage to do it? I often wondered if there was something different about her generation or if there was something wrong with me!

One day when I was feeling particularly frustrated, I let it spill out. "Mom, you can do anything," I told her. "I wish I could do half the things that you do so well. You are always so calm and in control."

"I learned it the hard way," she replied with a smile. "The war made us very self-reliant. When I was eighteen years old, I left home and escaped to Russia. I never saw my parents again. Facing the dangers of wartime in a strange country forced me to tackle many problems, and it took a lot of strength to survive. Later, when it was all over, we just didn't get excited over the *kleinikeiten,* the trivial things in life." My mother ended with a blessing that Hashem should protect me so that I would never have to learn by experience how to endure hardship.

We children did not suffer any of the serious troubles that our parents had, thank G-d, but they did try in their own way to prepare us to handle life. One of their main strategies was not to give in to all of our demands, so we did grow up relatively unspoiled. But even though I absorbed my parents' values, I still found that I had to learn many coping skills along the way. There were times when I simply did not feel equal to the tasks that faced me.

I kept wondering: Is the hard way the *only* way to learn how to cope? Isn't there another way we can change our outlook on challenges? Yes, that first *Shabbos* meal I had made was quite a fiasco, but with time my cooking improved. Wasn't it possible that coping might simply be another skill that could be learned just as we learn how to cook?

Are you thinking to yourself, "It's not that simple"? Have you read other books about personal development? Have you found that once you finished the book you would soon go back to your usual way of coping, and all the negative traits you were trying to avoid would creep back in? I have found that the questions in many of these books are better than the answers. The books promise great results, but the suggestions they give are often unrealistic in practice.

In order to experience *real* change, all we have to do is turn to the *real* source — the Torah itself. Everything we need to know is in the Torah, and its recommendations are universally effective. If we use them properly, we really *can* learn how to stop a bad habit. We really *can* learn how to make difficult decisions. We really *can* learn to overcome disappointment and to serve Hashem with enthusiasm.

People often ask me where my ideas come from. They want to know if these concepts will only help strong-willed or talented people to improve, or if they will work for ordinary people too. And so I tell them that the "professional advice" in this book came straight from ordinary people, just like themselves. The recipes that are offered here have been tested in the "kitchen" of real life.

Over the years I have spoken with dozens of women who made changes in their lives. I interviewed them by phone, visited and observed them in person, and wrote them letters filled with questions. There was a magnetic force that drew me to these unsung heroines. Each one had a special nobility. I collected the bits of wisdom that these women had shared with me and organized them into a system. Gradually the project grew until it developed into a lecture series. I offered this system for growth to several different groups. The techniques were simple, yet they worked; people walked out smiling.

I began to think how wonderful it would be if I could share these ideas with a wider audience and help even more people to cope with the trials of daily life. And so the book was born.

The people you will meet in these stories have actually practiced the Torah concepts outlined in the following pages, and they have developed the confidence and strength to improve their lives. They have displayed simple wisdom, self-control, and extraordinary kindness. Many of them had a valid reason to be miserable, and yet they were not. Some were struggling with pain, but they worked hard to grow spiritually and to give to others. One woman began to bake *challah* regularly. Another organized *Sheva Brachos* for an orphan, and a third found the courage to break the negative pattern of interaction in her family. Each of their accomplishments, no matter how small it may have appeared outwardly, was a personal triumph. Each new achievement gave them a sense of pride and the encouragement to go further.

And the best part is that they were all ordinary women, like you. They challenged the attitudes that made them feel worthless and so can you.

The Chafetz Chaim, in *Give Us Life*, says that the light of Torah causes the darkness in our lives to fade away. He reminds us that we cannot drive darkness away by attacking it with weapons, but that if we light a single candle, the darkness will disappear by itself.

This book will show you how to light a candle. It will show you how to take small steps toward growth and will offer you exercises to do along the way that will give you a feeling of progress. Rabbi Samson Raphael Hirsch explains that a feeling of progression is synonymous with happiness, because the Hebrew word for happiness *simchah* is related to the word *tzemichah,* meaning growth. We do not need to be finished to feel fulfilled; we simply need to be on the way.

Imagine that you are standing at the corner, waiting for the tour bus to arrive. There is a wonderful feeling surging in you, the feeling that something good is about to happen.

This book is the tour bus. It will take its passengers as far as they want to go.

My Goals in This Workshop

Here is a list of the areas we will be working on in this book. Use numbers to indicate which areas you would most like to work on, in order of priority.

- ☐ FOCUS ON THE POSITIVE IN MYSELF
- ☐ FIND COURAGE TO TRY NEW THINGS
- ☐ KNOW WHAT TO DO WHEN I'M FEELING DOWN
- ☐ SET UP GOALS
- ☐ HAVE MORE BITACHON
- ☐ LEARN TO MAKE DECISIONS
- ☐ DO AWAY WITH A BAD HABIT
- ☐ SMILE MORE OFTEN
- ☐ HANDLE PROBLEMS WELL
- ☐ HAVE MEANINGFUL FRIENDSHIPS
- OTHER _____

Directions

In order to complete this book successfully, please:
1. *Read this book in order.*

If you skipped the introduction, read it now. Knowing the sources for the advice in the book will help you to feel secure that this system will work.

2. *Read the book in your favorite room.*

Comfortable surroundings are conducive to concentration and will make the mental exercise more pleasant.

3. *Make the lesson a priority.*

You don't have to hire a baby sitter, and you don't have to travel for three hours — but you do have to arrange not to be interrupted by the phone or visitors. Cook supper before you sit down to read and do not take out your knitting until you finish.

4. *Be kind to your heart — use the steps.*

Have you ever seen a sign near an escalator that read: "Be kind to your heart. Use the steps"? When the magic escalator steps carry you, you reach the end quickly, but if you want to grow, you have to use the muscles of your own mind. Do the exercises. They are easy and will not take a lot of time. If you glance at them and say, "I'll do this later," you are missing out on the main advantage of this book.

If you have enough willpower, do the exercises before you read the "True Responses" so that your thinking will not be influenced by other people's suggestions.

5. *Take short breaks.*

Your retention will be better if you pause and rest at the end of each chapter. Review the material in your mind. Take a walk around the room or around the block.

6. *Make an earnest effort.*

Success has less to do with the actual ability than with your desire and determination. You do not have to do a lot, but your effort must be sincere. In *Iyov* (17:9) we are told: וּטְהָר יָדַיִם יֹסִיף אֹמֶץ, *Hashem promises that when one earnestly attempts to come close to Him, He will give him the capacity to succeed.*

Enjoy!

PART I: FOCUSING ON THE POSITIVE

Chapter 1

> *Happiness or satisfaction in life does not depend on external circumstances, on things outside our minds. Our happiness does not depend on treasures that pass and escape us. It is in each person's heart . . . The tunes of truth, beauty, good, and righteousness play through our souls. Every physical thing that people think is wonderful and enjoyable passes like a fleeting shadow. The recognition that everything is dependent on our thoughts and not on outside circumstances is the key to one's emotional health. Physical health depends on one's emotional health.*
>
> (Rambam, quoted in *HaMafte'ach L'Osher HaChaim*)

Appreciating the "Little Things"

> *Whenever your mind is free, make a conscious effort to focus on the good that the Almighty has bestowed upon you.* (R' Bachya Ibn Pekuda)

Focusing on the gifts we have been given is something we have been encouraged to do since we were very young. But when problems preoccupy us or we feel pressured by circumstances, we often find it hard to be thankful for the things we most often take for granted: walking, talking, and the ability to accomplish daily tasks.

I learned a great deal about appreciation from a wonderful neighbor I once had.

When my husband and I were first married, we lived in an apartment in a semi-detached private house. The front porch was as large as our dining room, and the landlord had constructed a high, white iron railing, which ensured that the children could safely run and play there. We were only a stone's throw from the two couples who lived in the next house. The four families sat outside together in the summer evenings, sharing each other's company. My toddler drove his Big Wheel around the porch while my one-year-old played in a playpen. The adults talked, played Rummikub, read books, or did needlepoint. The evenings were very pleasant.

Actually, we were quite lucky. My children had two sets of "foster" grandparents — my landlords and the couple next door, Shmuel and Olga. These wonderful neighbors entertained the children whenever I had to run into the house to check on supper or to answer the phone. When the kids were finicky, "Uncle" Shmuel could always coax them to eat.

I could not go for walks on *Shabbos* because my younger child was still crawling, but on the long *Shabbos* afternoons in the spring and summer, I sat outside on the porch and enjoyed my neighbors' company. As we shared *Shalosh Seudos* meals with Olga and her husband, we talked and I learned. They shared their stories of survival in World War II and of their lives as pioneers in Israel; discussed their feelings and opinions about current events; and let me practice my lectures on them.

Olga has multiple sclerosis. At that time she walked with a walker by moving her hips and had use of only one hand. One afternoon when I came out to the porch with my children, her husband greeted us and said, "Aunt Olga is on her way." He said this because Olga's walk to the front porch from her kitchen took her ten minutes. I could hear the walker's rhythmic thumping on the floor. When Olga reached the porch, she looked at me brightly and said, "Hello! You look really nice today."

That is Olga. She is not bitter and does not complain. She is always smiling. People like her company, which is why she has lots of visitors. On Shabbos there are never fewer than six visitors at a time; there always seems to be a party on her porch. Her friends know they can always find her at home, ready to cheer them up and listen to their difficulties.

"Olga, you look nice too," I said, returning the compliment. "I like your earrings."

"The earrings were a gift from my daughter. I used to wear pierced earrings, but I always had to wait for my daughter to come and put them on for me. Now I've begun wearing clip earrings, which I can put on with one hand."

Many people in Olga's position would have given up long ago. Yet Olga tenaciously holds on to a normal life. Her appearance is impeccable. She won't even give up on her earrings.

I once came home from a shopping trip and found Olga busily scrubbing the porch floor. She had two buckets before her, one containing the sudsy water and one the clean water. She washed and rinsed one three-foot area at a time and then moved to a different spot. In that way she mopped the entire floor from her wheelchair.

"Olga," I said, "your porch floor is cleaner than my kitchen floor."

Olga replied with a smile, "My husband left on a long trip today, so I took the opportunity to do some work. He's always telling me I shouldn't strain myself."

My curiosity got the better of me one day, and I finally had to find out what Olga's secret was. "How is it," I asked her, "that despite your illness you have so many friends and are so cheerful?"

Olga refused to take the credit. "I only know nice people, so it's easy to be nice to them."

I knew better; I was Olga's neighbor, and some of her visitors were downright nuisances. "Olga, I won't mention names, but you somehow bring out the best in many people," I said.

"I guess I decided a long time ago to appreciate whatever I have," said Olga. "You have to look down and see those who have less than you. If you look up to those who have more, you won't be happy."

Olga then told me one of her wonderful stories. "A few years ago after an examination, I was wheeled out to the waiting room in the doctor's office, and I began to cry. A young girl in her twenties was sitting there. She asked me why I was crying.

" 'It's so hard,' I told her. 'When I look at the charts, I see how much my condition has deteriorated since last year. I was able to do so much more then.'

" 'Were you always sick?' she asked.

" 'No, it began about eight years ago.'

" 'Did you ever get married?'

" 'Sure,' I said. 'I have a loving husband, two children, and several grandchildren, thank G-d.'

" 'Did you ever have a job?' the girl continued.

" 'Oh, yes! I used to design hats. I loved my work.'

" 'If you cry, what should I say?' asked the young girl. 'I probably will never be able to do any of those things.'

"This young girl showed me that although I thought I was in the worst possible position, I still enjoyed things that others don't have," Olga concluded.

Then she added an additional insight. "Another thing I've decided is that you can't expect people to like you. You have to work on liking *them*. A nurse came to help me out recently. I couldn't wait for her to like me — I had to be nice and to appreciate her first.

"Oh, one more thing. I am never disappointed, only pleasantly surprised. I don't say to a visitor, 'Oh, so you finally reminded yourself to come see me after six months!' I say instead, 'It's so nice to see you. Such a pleasant surprise!' "

Whenever I start to feel pressured, I think of Olga and I smile. What do I have to worry about? How bad can my present disappointment possibly be? Imagine how much easier it would be to pick up the toys if you said, "Thank you, Hashem," each time you bent down. "Thank you, I can bend my knees. Thank you, I can stand. It's tiring to bend, but I'm grateful that it doesn't hurt." When you feel grateful for the

Chapter One □ 25

little things that really mean so much, you can smile and relax.

> *Our sages say, "Who is the wealthy man who can boast of his riches? He who has a good heart and rejoices with the lot that Hashem has given him, wanting nothing more than he has." Such a person lives happily all his life, and he is able to serve Hashem properly.*
>
> *When a person is not satisfied with what he has, he constantly becomes weaker, and his soul is torn asunder when he sees others who have more than he. This is enough to drive a person out of this world... A person who is satisfied with what he has in life is blessed in this world; he does not need help from anyone. He is also blessed in the World to Come.*
> (MeAm Lo'ez, Avoth 4:1)

What is a practical and easy way to begin appreciating the "little things"? I'd like to offer the gratitude exercise that follows. It is suggested by Rabbi Zelig Pliskin in *Gateway to Happiness*. A friend and I tried it together and found that not only did it make us a little more grateful, it also provided great relaxation.

Exercise With Every Breath

The *Midrash* (*Bereishis Rabbah* 14:11) says that with every single breath we breathe, we should express our gratitude to the Almighty. As an exercise, put aside a five-minute period each day to be grateful for each breath.

Sit back comfortably, close your eyes, and take a deep breath. Imagine each breath nourishing your system. Let the air you breathe spread through your face and neck. As you slowly inhale, your arms and hands will feel stronger. Now, as you exhale, your arms and hands relax. Allow the tension to drain from your face and thank Hashem for each breath. Thank Him, too, that air is free. With your eyes still closed, slowly stretch. Listen to the quiet in the room. Sigh and take a few more deep breaths. Open your eyes.

Chapter 2

> רַבִּי שִׁמְעוֹן אוֹמֵר: וְאַל תְּהִי רָשָׁע בִּפְנֵי עַצְמֶךָ
> *Do not be wicked in your own estimation.*

(*Avos* 2:18)

Appreciating Yourself — There Will Never Be Another You

You have just found out that appreciating small things can be a very pleasant and accessible experience. In this chapter we will discuss another very vital form of appreciation: appreciation of yourself.

You are special. You have intrinsic worth, and you are a good person. Knowing this is the foundation of your growth.

Sometimes we doom ourselves to failure because we have unrealistic ambitions. We continually criticize ourselves because we have taken on more than we can realistically handle, and because we expect ourselves to be someone we aren't. Most people leave school with wonderful fantasies about the perfect lives they will lead, and when the real world doesn't measure up, they blame themselves. But these assumed inadequacies are in our minds.

Let me tell you about Esty. The first time I met her, she was holding a microphone and announcing the grand prize for the raffles at the annual tea of a national women's organization. You could taste the enthusiasm and friendliness in her voice, and she spoke as though she were in her own living room. The three hundred women in the room did not prevent Esty from being herself.

I asked Esty if she had any particular philosophy that gave her the ability to appear so much at ease in public. Her answer displayed a healthy and realistic attitude toward being human. She told me that she worked constantly at smoothing out her own rough edges, but at the same time she accepted not being perfect. "That's part of the territory," she said.

Even Esty's home reflected her matter-of-fact outlook on life. The house was very pleasant and well kept, but many of the kitchen fixtures had been purchased second hand. Esty had had to choose between a brand-new kitchen and putting in a laundry room, and she opted for the latter because it was functional and would make her day-to-day life more convenient. Esty did not berate herself about the impression her second hand kitchen would make on others, any more than she berated herself for not being perfect; to her, a functional house was more important than impressions. She accepted things as they were.

Esty continued with some important advice: "Don't measure yourself against other people. Don't carry a ruler in your head. Sometimes you go to a wedding or a *Bar Mitzvah*, and as soon as you enter the room you begin to measure. 'Is my dress too dressy or too casual? Is someone else wearing the same thing?

Are my shoes right? That woman near the table has the same *sheitel* as me, but mine is styled better thank goodness!' Well, these comparisons are not helpful."

Esty's ideas made me realize how often I had let this quiet voice inside me undermine my own serenity. I discovered that I was not alone. Many people carry an imaginary measuring stick in their minds, and sometimes the "stick" is on duty all day long. It is this stick that makes us run to clean up the house when unexpected visitors are about to show up, because we are sure the house will reflect poorly on us. It is the stick that makes us feel self-conscious when we can't get the stroller through the door, convinced that everyone is staring at us and thinking about what a *shlemazel* we are. And it is this same stick that makes us compare our children to others by trying to find out how everyone else is doing in school.

In order to give up these comparisons, it is essential to understand that Hashem intended everyone to be different. He did not want you to be exactly like the lady who lives next door. In fact, you are so unique that there will never be a person in history who is just like you.

In *Alei Shur,* Rav Shlomo Wolbe says that each person has been given the appropriate tools to fulfill his very individual mission:

> Each morning in the blessing "She'asah li kal tzarchi" we thank G-d for granting us everything we need to serve Him. We are prepared to accomplish our life tasks... Hashem doesn't want everyone to look at life in the same way and to learn and comprehend identically.

Rav Wolbe illustrates his point with the following story:

> Rav Naftali Amsterdam once said to his Rebbe, Rav Yisrael Salanter: "If only I had the head of the Sha'agas Aryeh, and the heart of the Yesod Veshoresh HaAvodah, and the great character of Rav Yisrael Salanter. Then I would be able to serve Hashem."

> *Rav Yisrael answered him: "Naftali, with your mind and your heart and your character, you can also be a true servant of Hashem."*

This is what we have to know," concludes Rav Wolbe. "There will never be another person in history, born in this place to these particular parents, with this unique combination of talents. We must serve Hashem with our mind and our heart and our abilities. There will never be another you."

When we discussed this idea at one of the workshops, one woman asked, "Isn't there a positive type of comparing?"

Yes, I told her, there was, and I read the women the following passage from *Pele Yo'eitz:*

When women meet, they can strengthen each other. By comparing their situations, they can learn to be better people. A woman can teach her friend about fearing Hashem. Instead of speaking slander and telling jokes, they can speak about how to be organized to serve Hashem; about prayers and halachos; and about how to raise their children and increase the harmony in their homes.

Turning off the negative "measuring stick" is not a difficult thing to do once we become aware of our thought patterns. It requires the simple act of taking our minds off the things we don't like about ourselves and focusing instead on the positive, however miniscule they may appear right now! Rather than asking ourselves self defeating questions like, "Why do I put things off?" or "Why can't I be like so-and-so?" we can concentrate instead on the good qualities that we do have, on the small achievements which are rightfully ours.

The source for this type of thinking is in the writings of David *Hamelech*. David wrote Chapter 36 of *Tehillim* as a song of praise to Hashem for helping him triumph over his evil inclination. In it, he describes in great detail the tempting talk of the *Yetzer Hara* as it prepares to shoot poisonous arrows into the innocent person's heart. This song of praise describes David's gratitude for every small triumph, each of which he considered an actual miracle (*Malbim,* Chapter 36).

David's spiritual struggle was far more intense than that of an ordinary person. This psalm is a heartfelt song of gratitude for his victories over the *Yetzer Hara* (*Alshich* on Chapter 36, quoted by ArtScroll *Tehillim*).

A few of the women in the workshop had contributions to make to this topic even before we did the exercise. They recognized the enormous value of small advances.

Leah said, "I passed a construction worker laying asphalt on a new road. I asked him, 'Will the road be much better?' He replied, 'Yes, it will be better, but *much* better is too much.'"

Shani said, "When I watch the everyday successes of my children, I learn how to appreciate doing something a little better than I had done it before. My son was playing an electronic game one day. He ran in, waving it like a flag, and called out, 'Look, Mommy, I beat my score!' If such a small thing could make him feel so good, then it could work for me too."

Are you ready to feel good about yourself, even though you are not perfect? Then let's focus on the positive.

Exercise: Five Things I Did Right Today

Write down five things you did right today. Enjoy those small steps in *Avodas Hashem* and thank Hashem that you succeeded.

1. _____

2. _____

3. _____

4. _____

5. _____

This exercise can give you a better opinion of those around you as well!

What are five things your child (or sister, or husband, or mother-in-law) did right today?

1. _____

2. _____

3. _____

4. _____

5. _____

Chapter 2: Five Things I Did Right Today
True Responses

The sentiment at the end of this lecture was markedly different from the beginning. The women had hesitated to participate. Not one of them believed that her "ordinary day" could inspire anyone else. After the session, though, everyone was smiling.

When I had said, "Let's write down five things we have done right today," there was an audible collective sigh and a rumble of bleak responses.

"I can't remember even one thing."

"Wow, five is a lot."

"I guess I'm not used to thinking of things I've done that were good."

"I'm going to have to think hard."

After a few moments, one little white card made its way to the front of the room, and several others followed. They were all filled in. You could see a sparkle in the women's eyes. A door had been opened through which they saw themselves in a different light.

One older woman, whose friend had brought her to the lecture from a nearby nursing home, had a suggestion to make: "Do you think we can plan ahead and set up five goals the day before, or would that be cheating?"

I asked around; the response was supportive. Most of the

ladies agreed that sticking to pre-established goals would be an even bigger success.

This woman's face glowed. She already had one item to mark down that evening on her list of five: Her advice had been accepted, and she felt special.

Here are some examples of "things done right" from the cards that were handed in at that workshop. Some of them may seem quite small, but each of them is valuable.

Five Things I Did Right Today

A

1. I called my friend who is not well, spoke to her, and wished her well.
2. I wrote a letter to my son and his family.
3. I woke my grandchildren on time for school.
4. I baked a cake for the friend who is ill.
5. I came to the lecture tonight.

B

1. I gave my son the time I had promised him, even though I was tempted to get side-tracked. It meant saying "no" to someone else.
2. Someone asked me for advice about the boy she was dating, and instead of thinking I knew all the answers, I helped her get in touch with her own feelings which is all she really wanted anyway.
3. Did seating for my son's *Bar Mitzvah*. I really made an effort to seat everyone with people they would feel comfortable with.
4. I finally made the decision to give our *yeshivah* the page in the journal and wrote down that we would come to the dinner.
5. I made chocolate *tefillin* for the *Bar Mitzvah* and didn't end up eating the chocolate!

C

1. I talked with someone who was lonely.
2. I participated in the women's tea for the *yeshivah*.

3. I helped my child with his homework.
4. I bought medicine that we need.
5. I greeted an angry lady politely.

D
1. I decided to make a birthday cake for my son at 12 o'clock last night.
2. I listened to Torah Tapes.
3. I visited a lonely neighbor.
4. I said *Tehillim.*
5. I learned about the *Parshah* of the week with a telephone partner.

E
1. I used my free time when both children were sleeping to make a fresh vegetable soup, which my husband loves.
2. I *davened Shacharis*.
3. I called a widow.
4. I wrote a letter to the Jewish Press, asking them to publish an appeal for volunteers to help the family of a retarded child.
5. I invited guests for supper.

F
1. I went to meet my three-year-old grandson's bus.
2. I told a lady who is house-bound about a telephone program which is run by an organization for the elderly.
3. I watched the baby for a little while.
4. I offered a drink to a charity collector who came to the door.
5. I *davened* and said *Tehillim.*

G
1. I decided to see a small project to completion, without loose ends. I cleared the table, washed the dishes, and put *everything* away.
2. Called my grandparents.
3. Did not act grouchy when my husband came home at 11:30 at night.
4. Took my friend's kids to the park.
5. Was firm with my son about going to sleep.

This exercise can be done by people of any age, as you will see below. When seniors in a girls' high school were asked to list any kind act they had done on a given day, their responses were varied and heartwarming. They included things that anyone can do, but most importantly, they remind us that small things are really big and deserve to be on the list.

Here is the "younger version" of this exercise:

Five Things I Did Right Today: Part 2

A
1. I gave up my lunch hour to type a report for a classmate. She types very slowly, and it would have taken her hours to complete.
2. I called a principal in another school to help one of my friends get a job for next year.
3. I stayed home for first period to help my mother. She's not feeling well, and she needed me to get the younger children off to school.
4. I smiled at a girl in a younger grade. She felt like a million dollars.

B
1. I spent the night studying with my friend. I would have finished much quicker on my own. It took a long time because I did a lot of explaining and teaching.
2. I was walking when I noticed a group of girls standing around a "slow" girl and taunting her. I told them that they were big girls and should not do this. They walked away.
3. I went to *shul* to answer to *Kaddish* and say *Amen*. I had a good feeling when I did this.

C
1. The new counselors in our day camp had a hard time in the beginning with their large group of very young children. I helped them for a week without getting paid.

2. I was looking forward to a dance class for seven weeks. Just as I was about to leave, my mother said that she would like to go. She went while I watched my little brother.
3. I saw a woman who looked like she'd had a hard day. She was shouting for her children to come to supper, but they were obviously ignoring her. I ran down the hill and brought them home. The mother didn't have enough words to thank me.

Chapter 3

> In Iyov (26:7) we are told: תּוֹלֶה אֶרֶץ עַל־בְּלִימָה.
> The simple meaning is that the world hangs in midair;
> there is nothing holding it in place as it revolves in space.
> But there is a deeper meaning given by the Sages:
>
> אָמַר ר׳ אִילְעָא: אֵין הָעוֹלָם מִתְקַיֵּם אֶלָּא בִּשְׁבִיל מִי שֶׁבּוֹלֵם אֶת עַצְמוֹ בִּשְׁעַת מְרִיבָה. שֶׁנֶּאֱמַר: תּוֹלֶה אֶרֶץ עַל בְּלִימָה.
>
> The world is held up by one who keeps quiet at a time of quarrel. He is the one who could have been aggressive when he was wronged but instead resolved the problem without producing enmity.
>
> *(Chullin 89:1)*

Appreciating Others

We have spoken about developing appreciation for the "small things" in life, and we've tapped the topic of being more generous toward yourself. But there is still one more area in which a good attitude can actually save the world: the way in which we relate to others.

Do you ever feel distant from people you would like to befriend? Do you ever feel too shy to approach or help someone you don't know well? Are you quick to make assumptions about other people's actions and slow to forgive hurts? This chapter will help you to break down some of those walls.

Before we begin, try taking the following quiz. It will help you pinpoint where you fall in the "comfort scale" of relationships with others and may provide you with clues about why you react the way you do in interpersonal situations.

Quiz: How Comfortable Are You With People?

1. What happens when you find yourself facing someone you have never met before?
    a. I feel uncomfortable and want to hide.
    b. I look the other person over carefully to make sure that her hairstyle, clothing, and shoes are not quite as good as mine.
    c. I look straight at the other person and let my eyes meet hers.
2. You are participating in a parenting workshop and you have described a problem you are having with your child. How do you feel when someone recounts how she handled that same problem skillfully?
    a. Threatened
    b. Embarrassed
    c. Interested
3. You owe someone a thank-you note. How will you send one?
    a. I buy one with a printed message in the store.
    b. I quickly toss off a few standard lines because the recipient will probably just throw it away anyway.
    c. I invest effort and thought and try to write something personal that expresses my true feelings.
4. You hear that your favorite high school teacher is visiting from Israel. You have not spoken to her for ten years. What do you do?
    a. I would not call because I'd feel too shy.
    b. I would not call because she probably forgot who I am.

      c. I would call to tell her that I still remember some of the ideals she taught and that I wanted to thank her.
5. When someone is angry at you and you don't think that anything you say will help, what do you do?
      a. I feel guilty but do nothing.
      b. I let my anger out and make it clear to the other person how wrong he/she was.
      c. I prepare a special gift for the person who is angry.
6. Your close friend's grandson is getting married. Although the grandmother told you that she hopes to see you at the wedding, her children never sent you an invitation. What do you do?
      a. I would feel distressed. I would assume that my friend changed her mind about me and told her children not to send the invitation.
      b. I would call my friend and openly tell her how indignant I am about not being invited.
      c. I would assume the missing invitation was a mistake. I'd go to the *chupah* and wish my good friend *Mazel Tov*.
7. As you are about to leave the house, your adolescent daughter criticizes what you are wearing and says, "I don't want any of my friends to see you in the street." What do you do?
      a. I would feel horrible. I would think that I failed as a mother.
      b. We would probably start shouting, and I'd point out all of my child's faults to her.
      c. I would not do anything that minute, but at a quieter, calmer moment several hours later, I would explain to my daughter that although she can tell me her feelings, they must be said with respect.
8. You are riding in a minivan with twelve other passengers. Suddenly you begin to feel nauseated and need air. What do you do?
      a. I would never be able to admit that I need to have the window open. I would suffer for the rest of the trip.

      b. I would open the window without asking, and if anyone complained, I would feel frustrated that no one had noticed my discomfort earlier.

      c. I would explain the situation briefly, ask if anyone would mind if I opened the window, and take action.

9. Your husband tells you he has a skin infection that has bothered him for some time.
    a. I would feel overwhelmed by the problem. I would start thinking about all the negative aspects of his condition and what I would have to do.
    b. I would point out that he brought this all on himself because he should be taking better care of himself.
    c. I would encourage him to look for possible solutions and offer my help without insisting.
10. It is one A.M. and your child has been crying for several hours with an earache. You call the doctor, but he says he can only help you in the morning. What do you do?
    a. I would feel embarrassed and helpless.
    b. I would decide that the doctor is cruel and unfeeling, and that I would never use him again.
    c. I would try once more to reach the doctor and politely explain the seriousness of the situation. If I could not get help from him, I would try another doctor.

    Now total your a's, b's, and c's.

    Seven or more a's means you may need to value yourself more.

    Seven or more b's means you may need to value others more.

Seven or more c's means you probably have a healthy balance. You respect yourself, and you also respect others.

    If you have fallen into the "a" range, there are steps you can take to feel more confident about approaching other people and to make interaction with them less traumatic. Keep reading.

Chapter Three □ 43

Defusing Interpersonal Tension

Very often we create distance between ourselves and those around us because of the mistake of not giving others the benefit of the doubt. We judge people too hastily, including members of our own family. It is amazing how much tension can be erased simply by assuming people innocent of our imagined charges.

> A king planted an orchard with perfect rows of figs, palms, grapevines, apples, and pomegranates. He put it in the care of a sharecropper and left. A while later the king returned to inspect his orchard and found it in ruins, full of thorns and brambles.
>
> As he was about to command his wood-choppers to chop down and destroy the desolate orchard, he spotted one beautiful rose among the briars. He took it and smelled it and calmed down, his soul refreshed. He declared, "Because of this rose, the entire orchard will be saved." (Midrash Vayikra Rabbah 23:3)

The rose in this parable refers to the person who maintains peace among his fellow men. G-d considers it worthwhile to save the entire orchard meaning, of course, the world for the sake of this precious keeper of the peace.

Rochel sells raffles for a yearly *tzedakah* party. Each year they call her a few weeks before the event to invite her to come and to give her the last-minute details. This year they did not call, and Rochel had no idea what to do. Her first thoughts were angry ones: Perhaps the committee had decided that she was not "good enough" for the honor of helping out and had given her job to someone else.

On the day of the party, Rochel's sister-in-law drove her to the hall and dropped her off. "You go in first, Rochel," she said. "I don't want to see what's going to happen."

Rochel took a deep breath and walked in. There were two people sitting at the raffle table. One was a woman she had worked with for several years now. This lady was not involved in the backstage workings of the organization and would probably assume that Rochel had been called back as usual.

The other woman looked as though she were just filling in. Rochel decided that neither of these people would mind if she helped out. So she took off her coat, walked behind the table, and began selling raffles.

When her sister-in-law walked in a few minutes later, she just stood and stared. "I can't believe it, Rochel," she finally said.

After Rochel told me this story, I asked her how she had managed to handle a potentially explosive situation in such a cool-headed manner.

"First, I gave everyone the benefit of the doubt," she told me. "I assumed it was probably just an oversight. Second, I asked myself what I was afraid of. Would someone tell me outright to get out because I was not supposed to be selling raffles? Of course not!

"The real icing on the cake came a few minutes later, when the president of the organization came over to me. She said, 'Oh, Rochel, we're so thankful that you came! It's been a hard year because Hindy was sick, and things just weren't as organized as usual. It wasn't until today that we realized we had forgotten to call you. We really didn't know how we would manage but now you're here!'

"Well, from now on I have a steady job sellling raffles," Rochel concluded with a smile of contentment.

Rochel, the heroine of this story, is one of those people who keeps the earth suspended in space. In her quiet way, she has become the rose in the king's garden, the one for whom Hashem upholds the world.

We can also give people the benefit of the doubt retroactively. Have you ever found that when you are involved in an argument with someone, most probably someone close to you, that you suddenly remember six other things this person "did" to you in the past? These are usually things which you thought were forgotten, and which have no bearing at all on the current problem. Past insults, imagined or not, have a tendency to build secure nests in our minds, unless we make a solid attempt to uproot them.

The following exercise will help you find ways to defuse potential bombs in an interpersonal situation, whether present or past.

Exercise Part 1: The Benefit Of The Doubt

1. Who are the significant people in your life?

_____

_____

_____

_____

2. List at least one good thing each of these people has done for you in recent years. Perhaps they didn't offer you support when you really wanted it. Nevertheless, it is most likely that they have given you support and praise at some other time but you have forgotten. By making a conscious effort to renew those positive experiences, you will feel better both about yourself and about others.

_____

_____

_____

_____

_____

_____

_____

_____

Part 1: Defusing Interpersonal Tension
True Responses

1. Someone offered me a ride and accidentally closed the door on my hand. The pain was excruciating and I felt a burst of anger inside, but the driver was expecting, and I didn't want to frighten her. In my softest voice I said, "My skirt is stuck and I can't reach the door handle. Could you open the car door, please?"
2. In ten minutes my aunt and uncle were arriving from New Jersey to visit. I was stirring the soup in the kitchen when I heard a loud crash in the living room. I pictured my living room floor filled with scattered glass fragments. My first instinct was to scream and yell and hit whichever child I could reach first. I told myself to calm down and look carefully at the room first and assess the damage. Luckily the crash was caused by a falling bucket of blocks.
3. Once again my client was late for our appointment. This would throw my entire schedule off. I pictured the complaints of ten dissatisfied customers and began to anticipate a really awful day. My ulcer began acting up. I reached into my pocketbook and took out my *Tehillim;* it felt good to be using my waiting time constructively. The *Tehillim* also helped me to keep a calm face when the client finally did show, and instead of picking a bone with her, I smiled and started styling her wig. About two hours later one of my other customers called to cancel, so the schedule evened out and my day wasn't that bad after all. Only two customers had to wait.
4. For a long time I avoided talking to my mother-in-law about a serious problem. I realized it was very important for me to keep the lines of communication open, and that continued delay just increased the bitterness between us. I felt it was right to air my grievances, but I took it slowly, bit by bit, and didn't blurt them all out at once like a little kid. I asked Hashem for help, and thank goodness it's working.

5. I agonized over a sister-in-law who kept bringing inappropriate toys as gifts for my son. Finally, I called last night and told my brother in the nicest way I could that the toys weren't helping Nochum to grow. He said it was no problem. I gave a few suggestions for appropriate toys, and even though I was frightened when I picked up the phone, it worked out okay.

6. The firm where I work is owned by Orthodox Jews, and we had always been paid for *Yom Tov* days which fell out in the middle of the week. One year I decided to take my vacation during *Succos*. I assumed that I could count five days of vacation, aside from the actual *Yom Tov* days themselves. But when I returned, I found I had been given a check for only half what I had expected. The loss of a week's salary was no small matter to me, especially since I wasn't prepared for it; it meant being in debt for a while, and I was really angry.

   I am very high-strung, and my tendency has always been to take an accusatory stance whenever I get the short end. But I decided this time to make a real effort to practice diplomacy. I called my boss aside, put on a calm although forced smile, and asked him quietly about the amount on the check, taking the attitude that perhaps it had been an oversight. He told me that *Yom Tov* days were not paid if vacation was taken in conjunction with them. No one had ever told me about this policy, and my indignation was growing steadily, but I maintained my composure.

   "This is really difficult for me," I told him. "I didn't know about the policy. One paycheck makes a big difference in my budget."

   "Remind me about this before *Pesach*," he said, "and we'll see what we can do to work around it next time."

   In my mind, I still felt that someone should have forewarned me, but I held my peace. I had really won a victory; the boss had acknowledged my loss and agreed to try and prevent another one in the future, and we were still on good terms.

7. My husband and I had been unable to come to an agreement over a fairly important issue for over a month. I was feeling very tense and angry, and I could feel that at any moment it might just come bursting out of me. One morning as I was cleaning up from breakfast, my husband came walking into the house and handed me a small paper bag. Inside was a chocolate cupcake, my favorite kind. I knew it had been difficult for him to do that, and it helped relax the atmosphere so that we could have a calm talk.

Part II: Breaking The Ice

We've already spoken about easing tension in relationships with people you already know. What about establishing new friendships?

Are you sometimes reluctant to approach people you don't know well or don't know at all because you are too shy or self-conscious? Have you passed up opportunities to be of service because you are not sure how people will react to you?

Seven years ago I was sitting on a charter bus that would take me from Jerusalem to Petach Tikva. My fellow passengers were all teachers and organizers who were on their way to an annual leadership convention. I sat next to a woman who was actively involved in introducing the *mitzvos* to secular women on kibbutzim. She was scheduled to give a talk that day at the convention about her techniques.

This woman began to describe how she knocks on the doors of people she has never met, talking casually with them for a while and trying to convince them to try an entirely different lifestyle. Her success rate is very high.

I took a second look at my neighbor. She was about fifty years old; she wore a simple dress and thick stockings, and a hat covered her wig. Her background was vastly different from that of the women she was dealing with. In fact, she lived in a tiny two-room apartment in the Old City and did not even have a phone.

"How do you do it?" I asked. "How do you reach through so

many barriers to women who have a totally alien life-style and succeed in drastically changing their lives?"

She told me that her answer could be found in the writings of Rav Mordechai Shulman of Slobodka, *zt"l*, who gives the following insight:

> *There seems to be a contradiction in the Nishmas prayer. On one hand, all the kindnesses of G-d bring one to the realization that thanks and gratitude are due only to Him. We go on to say that "even if our mouths were full of song like the sea, and our tongues full of hymns like the multitudes of waves, and our lips full of praise like the breadth of the sky" even with such an unimaginable range of powers, we would be unable to thank Him for even one of the many wonders which He has done for us.*
>
> *But in the same prayer we say that with our limbs and our tongues we shall praise Hashem! It appears that the mouth does have the power to express proper thanks and praise to G-d.*
>
> *Actually, there is no contradiction. It all depends on how we view the limbs of the body. If we view the mouth as "our mouth" and the tongue as "our tongue," then "we would be unable to praise." But when the limbs are those that Hashem has given us and the tongue is one which He has placed in our mouths — when the limbs of a person belong to G-d and are dedicated to His service then there is no limit to their strength.*

"I think of this Torah thought on the threshold of each home before I enter," my neighbor on the bus explained. "I consider my limbs and my mouth as being totally in the service of G-d. I never go into a house alone because Hashem is with me."

I looked at her radiant face and I envied her. She had taken a piece of spiritual insight which most of us would feel is beyond our grasp, and turned it into a simple, practical working tool.

Year after year we meet hundreds of people. There are some, like my neighbor on the bus, who leave a special impact on us, whose images generate a smile whenever we think of them. We wonder what makes them so easy to approach, and so comfortable in approaching others, and we probably imagine that they were born with this special knack for "breaking the ice." My guess is that they had to work on it, just like anyone else, one step at a time.

Here is an "icebreaker" that you may find helpful.

Exercise: Breaking The Ice

1. Everyone has an area of competence, even if it is not a professional skill. Some people can drive well, others can bake or sew, while others have an area of special knowledge. Your unique resources can help you break the ice and develop relationships.

    What are you good at?

    _____

    _____

    _____

    _____

2. Think of a way in which you can use your talent to help you become acquainted with someone you want as a friend.

    _____

    _____

    _____

    _____

    _____

    _____

Part 2: Breaking The Ice — True Responses

Here are some true stories of women who did not let their inhibitions take precedence over their desire to get involved with others. In all cases, the results were much better than they had expected.

1. I have lived alone for five years. Many times when I wake up in the morning, I feel a real need for some company, but I am too shy to call someone up out of the blue and ask her to come over to visit. Fortunately I drive a car; thanks to that, I can call and say, "I'm going shopping at the mall today would you like to join me?" I can always find someone who'd like to get out, and this way I have the pleasure of pleasant company for the afternoon.

2. A woman I know lives alone and recently broke her arm. I drive, so when I shopped for myself, I bought some basic groceries for her. I didn't ask her; I just went and did it because I knew she needed it.

3. Years ago, an acquaintance from my hometown in Brazil had a baby on *Succos*. We were now living in the same city but were rarely in touch. I knew that her parents still lived in Brazil, and since her oldest daughter was only five, she had no one to help out. On *Chol Hamoed*, I called and invited her five-year-old to come with us on a family outing. This woman and I have since become very close friends. The baby just had his *Bar Mitzvah* this year.

4. I go to a certain *shiur* every *Shabbos*. An elderly woman who lives on my block also attends every week, but at one point she suddenly stopped coming. For a week or two I hesitated; I really didn't know her, and I didn't want to hurt her feelings by asking any uncomfortable questions. Finally I got up the nerve and called. She said that she had fainted in the grocery store and was now afraid to walk out alone. I arranged to accompany her, and we walk together to the *shiur* every week now. We've been doing this for a few months.

5. My best friend's sister, Aliza, was in the same bungalow colony with us last summer. Although I was very close to her sister, I had never crossed her path at all. One morning I saw that her children were running around in pajamas at eleven o'clock. I asked them what happened, and they told me that their mother was sick in bed. I ran home and warmed up the extra cheese latkes from last night's supper and served the children breakfast. Then I asked the oldest child where everyone's clothes were and got them dressed. I sent this daughter in to tell her mother that I was taking the children to my bungalow.

   The next day when she felt better, Aliza came over to thank me. "I had an awful twenty-four-hour virus," she said. "I just couldn't move. I don't know what I would have done without your help. It's not that the people in the bungalows right near me didn't ask if they could do something, but I was too embarrassed to take them up on the offer. What made you do it?"

   I told her that three years ago I had been sick in the bungalow colony too, and no one had helped me. I was too embarrassed to say that I needed help, and my kids just stayed in pajamas all day. I promised myself then that if I ever saw someone else with that problem, even if I didn't know her well I'd make sure to help.

PART II: OVERCOMING OBSTACLES

How many times have you heard about something wonderful that a peer of yours has accomplished and thought, "Maybe I could do that too?"

How many times have you read a biography of a *tzaddik* and put it down with a big sigh?

How often have you dwelled on an unpleasant experience in your past and allowed it to determine what you will do or not do in the future?

Today, Orthodox women buy more *sefarim* in English than men, and yet, growth conscious as we are, we have barely scratched the surface of our potential. Perhaps this is because of some unchallenged assumptions we carry around. If we learn to think differently, we will have the courage to try new things.

In the first part of this section we will discuss a few myths that block our growth and find ways to overcome the discouragement and fear that sometimes overwhelm us. In the second part, we will attempt to set in motion some healthy patterns of activity that will gradually weaken the grip our negative thoughts have on us.

Chapter 4

> הוּא הָיָה אוֹמֵר: לֹא עָלֶיךָ הַמְּלָאכָה לִגְמוֹר, וְלֹא אַתָּה בֶן חֹרִין לְהִבָּטֵל מִמֶּנָּה
>
> *Do not be dismayed, says Rabbi Tarfon. "The work is not for you to complete." Your obligation is to study as much as you can and to learn as much as you can. In no sense do you have to finish the work. On the other hand, "you are not at liberty to desist altogether." As the Chafetz Chaim says, "It is not for you to achieve but to act. Achievement is the province of the Almighty."*
>
> (*Ethics from Sinai*, Irving Bunim; *Avos 2:21*)

The Opportunities We Miss

If you have been doing the exercises, you have discovered by now that your day is full of small accomplishments that you had never acknowledged before. You may even have begun to think about opening up in your relationships with other people. I hope that as you did a little introspection, you began to realize that those items were just the tip of the iceberg. You have so much more potential hidden within you.

While preparing to write this chapter, I heard a stomping

noise. I looked up to see my one-year-old son wobbling toward me in his big brother's shoes. The smile on his face expressed a mixture of anxiety and excitement. Those first steps proved that he could walk without holding on. I clapped and cheered him on.

Then my baby stopped. His face conveyed his thoughts so clearly: "Where am I? How did I get stranded in the middle of the room with nothing to hold on to? Why did I do this? I can't walk. I'll fall on my face." He promptly sat down. I walked over and tried to coax him to get up, but he refused. I knew he could do it; why had he stopped now?

What stops us from trying new things?

Do we say, "I just can't; I'll fall on my face"? Do we decide we can get by perfectly well without ever doing that particular thing? Do we feel that since we can't stretch, our goals will just have to shrink?

I know my baby can walk and try to coax him to try. G-d, too, knows that we can do great things and tries to coax us to go for it. G-d tells us (*Devarim* 14:1) every day, ... בָּנִים אַתֶּם לַה׳ אֱלֹקֵיכֶם וְאַתֶּם תִּהְיוּ־לִי מַמְלֶכֶת כֹּהֲנִים וְגוֹי קָדוֹשׁ, *You are My children . . . You will be a kingdom of priests and a holy nation to me* (*Shemos* 19:6).

But often we do not take Him up on his offer. We resort to a frugal spiritual diet, cutting out everything that could possibly be considered a "frill." This means that we avoid challenging ourselves spiritually because it is so much easier not to do the work and also because we are pretty sure we can't succeed. Why? Why live like a pauper when you are really a prince?

The Chafetz Chaim makes this point very clearly:

> *If you ask a businessman why he struggles so hard to avoid poverty when there are so many poor people in the world who get by, he will tell you that he doesn't want to be a pauper. So why are people willing to be paupers in Torah just because they can get by with a bare minimum of study?*
>
> (Chafetz Chaim, *Give Us Life*)

It is very frustrating to have a strong urge to do something — something noble and big, or even something that is simply novel for you and then to feel stopped in your tracks. Sometimes an idea suddenly pops up inside you, like a tulip in a spring garden. It may have been triggered by someone you know who made a suggestion, by a book you read, or by an inspiring lecture.

However, you put off doing anything. The ideal that was strong and vibrant starts to weaken and diminish but it doesn't entirely disappear. It stays inside and occasionally springs up again. Where does it come from?

אָמַר רַב יְהוֹשֻׁעַ בֶּן לֵוִי: בְּכָל יוֹם וָיוֹם בַּת קוֹל יוֹצֵאת מֵהַר חוֹרֵב וּמַכְרֶזֶת וְאוֹמֶרֶת: ,,אוֹי לָהֶם לַבְּרִיּוֹת מֵעֶלְבּוֹנָהּ שֶׁל תּוֹרָה"

The Baal Shem Tov says that the voice inside you is a *Bas Kol,* a heavenly voice. Every day it echoes from Mount Sinai and calls us to follow the Torah. Every person you learn from and every incident you observe is an echo of the heavenly voice rousing you to action.

(*Baal Shem Tov* on *Pirkei Avos* 6:2)

How can we find a way to answer that voice without getting stopped in our tracks?

The following exercises will help you to get in touch with the feelings of anxiety you have when an opportunity presents itself and you feel reluctant to accept the challenge. Later, we will move on to practical remedies.

Exercise No. 1: The "Missed Boat"

You are caught in the middle of a valley between two mountains. On one mountain there is a small voice saying, "Come on, you can," and on the other side a more insistent voice calling out, "No, you can't." You turn your head to one side and then to the other. Which way should you go? If you climb the "safe" mountain and remain with the status quo, you may never reach your goal. Will you take the risk of pursuing a dream, knowing that you will find it hard to return to your safe cocoon again? Which direction will you choose?

The first step toward overcoming obstacles to change is to think about why we avoid opportunities in the first place. These questions may require a little soul-searching. Take your time. This book is your private forum, and it is all right to write down anything you wish.

1. How did you feel when you saw a possibility that you knew you could act on — but did not?

___

___

___

2. Why do you think you avoided the change?

___

___

___

3. What were the benefits of not "rocking the boat"?

___

___

___

4. How would you have benefited if you had taken the challenge?

___

___

___

Chapter Four □ 61

Write down whatever ideas come to you. After you finish, put the book down and take a short rest. You might want to walk around the room or just close your eyes for a few minutes. When you feel ready, continue to the second part of the exercise.

Exercise No. 2: "One of These Days"

Think of something you have dreamed of doing for some time. Do you want to find time for more learning or teaching? Do you want to pray with more sincerity or to develop more faith? Do you want to work on being kinder to other people?

Whatever your choice, please keep four things in mind:
1. It is very tempting to solve our problems by working on someone else's growth. Don't write in, "I'd like to make my husband come home on time."
2. Choose something that is dependent on your actions. Don't write, "One of these days I'd like to win the lottery."
3. Make the goal limited in scope. Be fair to yourself.
4. Pick something *you* really want to do, not something you feel obligated to do to please others.

Keep in mind that there are no right or wrong answers in this exercise, no excuses too "silly." Your problems are very real, and they are important. It is okay to have a look at them.

One of these days I would like to. . .

_____

_____

_____

_____

But I cannot because...

1. _____

2. _____

3. _____

4. _____

5. _____

6. _____

7. _____

8. _____

Chapter 3: "One Of These Days" True Responses

In this particular workshop, the process of identifying potential goals was gratifying, even before any attempt was made to find a solution. The women in the group learned that some of them had common dreams, and that helped them feel closer to one another. It was encouraging to find that they were pulling together in the same direction.

Another immediate benefit was that people offered to help others reach their goals. There was an incredible pool of resources. Last but not least, there was a sense of reassurance, because some items considered overwhelming by one person were easier for the next, thus giving everyone a feeling of competence in some area.

Here are some typical group responses. See if you can find yourself among them!

ONE OF THESE DAYS I'D LIKE TO...	BUT I CANNOT BECAUSE...
Start a home-study program, a yeshiva without walls.	I lack the ability, organization, and patience to work on it.
Change jobs.	I'm afraid to walk out on a secure situation, even though I'm unchallenged. I worry a lot about money.
Stop speaking lashon hara.	People will feel insulted when I tell them not to talk. I forget the halachos. I hesitate to ask a Rav what's permissible. My family will think I'm being extreme.
Listen to more Torah tapes.	I spend time listening to other people, but I really need more time for myself. I'm tired. I need to be more organized to fit it in.
Finish the book I began writing.	I can't find the time. I lose confidence when I start a project. Other things keep coming up which seem more important. I'm too tired. I get my best ideas when I'm doing something else.
Learn more prayers by heart.	I have a bad memory!

Did any of your answers match the examples you have read here? It is a good feeling to see that you are not alone.

I have saved my best "true response" for last. This person was not in the workshop, but he had at least six reasons why he considered his task impossible. Can you guess who said it?

> When I began to act upon my decision to write this book I realized that a person like me is not capable of authoring this work. After I evaluated myself, I decided

I could not organize the material properly. I do not have the patience for this; I do not know the Arabic language well, yet I want to write in Arabic because it is the prevalent language today. I am afraid to put such tremendous effort into something that will be hard to complete. Maybe this work is inappropriate for me.

I have decided to stop the project completely.

The person who wrote this passage was the eleventh century Spanish *Gaon*, Rabbeinu Bachya, son of Rabbi Yosef Ibn Pekuda. He did manage to overcome his concerns and authored the classic *Chovos HaLevavos*. His work has survived the wanderings and upheavals of the Jewish People over the last 950 years.

You can see from this story that none of us is above self doubt. But that does not mean we cannot move on and get things done.

Chapter 5

> There was a man who urgently needed to speak with the Rebbe, but whenever he was with him, he could not open his mouth. He found it impossible to tell the Rebbe what was in his heart.
>
> One Friday afternoon the Rebbe said to him, "Make a habit of speaking to G-d. Then you will be able to speak to me."
>
> The man followed his advice and was soon able to speak to the Rebbe, although he still found it very difficult to express himself.
>
> The Rebbe said, "You are like a warrior who arms himself and prepares to break down a mighty wall. When you come to the gate, you find it blocked with a spider web. Can you imagine anything more foolish than returning in defeat because of a spider web blocking your path?"

(from *Rabbi Nachman's wisdom*, translated by Rabbi Aryeh Kaplan)

Dispelling the Myths

Resistance to change has its roots deep in our mental habituation. Our hesitation stems partly from an underestimation of our abilities, and partly from some very firmly rooted assumptions that we carry around, assumptions that have no basis.

These false beliefs are the "cobwebs" that Rav Nachman is speaking of. The *Yetzer Hara* takes these cobwebs and enlarges them in our minds, making them seem bigger than they really are. He creates needless fear. A rational person knows that even though a cobweb may be unpleasant, there is no reason to be afraid of it; it is easily pushed aside.

In this chapter we will begin to tear down some of the crippling myths that impede our progress, and we will discover how insubstantial those "cobwebs" really were. Let's begin by bringing one of them to the surface right now. Answer the following questions as instinctively as you can.

True Or False

1. One's behavior patterns are inherited and cannot be changed.
   ☐ True   ☐ False
2. A *tzaddik* is sure that he is capable of great accomplishment. He never has doubts.
   ☐ True   ☐ False
3. Great men are so good because they only have a *Yetzer Tov*.
   ☐ True   ☐ False

Of course the answers to these questions are very simple in fact, almost embarrassingly so. But something keeps us from applying this knowledge to ourselves. As one workshop participant said, "We *know* what the answers are, but we *feel* the opposite." Let's take a look at each of these questions separately.

1. One's behavior patterns cannot be changed.

Can we alter our behavior patterns? Can we enjoy the feeling of accomplishment that comes with doing the right thing under trying circumstances? Can we still change now even though we are no longer in our "formative" years?

Many of the women in a recent workshop were hovering around the forty-year-old mark. Some of them were well-known figures in the Jewish community, yet they felt that they were missing out on something. As one said, "Some things I do very well; other things I botch up very well."

I was able to use their age to show them that change is indeed possible. I told them, "Don't give up. You may have followed one pattern for forty years, but you can still pursue another way now. Wasn't Rabbi Akiva an ignorant shepherd? At the age of forty, he began with the *Aleph Beis*. Yet he became the Torah giant of his generation. It's never too late to change."

Not only can one change, but Hashem helps and rewards those who develop the power to improve, even if it is at a later stage of life.

> The story is told that when Rabbi Eliezer once came forward to pray for rain on behalf of the Jews, he recited twenty-four blessings — and received no answer. Then Rabbi Akiva took his place and began to pray : "Avinu Malkeinu our Father, our King, we have no king but You. . ." Immediately he was answered. The people thought this was because Rabbi Akiva was greater than Rabbi Eliezer. However, a heavenly voice came forth and testified: "It is not because one is greater than the other, but because one transcends his own nature and the other does not."
>
> This distinction between the two sages is explained by the fact that Rabbi Eliezer was of noble lineage. A fine character was fostered in him by his environment and education. He therefore had no need to struggle against his own nature, to suppress old instincts, and to recreate himself.
>
> Rabbi Akiva, however, once said of himself, "Before I began studying Torah, I used to say, 'Find me a Torah sage, and I will bite him on the neck on Yom Kippur, just as a donkey bites.'" (Shabbos Shiurim, Parshas Ki Sisa, Rabbi M. Miller, Gateshead)

Rabbi Akiva had a great deal of work to do in refashioning his own character. It was because of his success in this formidable task of changing his own nature that Hashem responded in kind by changing the laws of nature and sending rain.

So the answer to question number one is FALSE: One's behavior patterns are not inherited, and they can be changed. Of course, no one expects you to change your nature overnight, or even by the time you reach the end of this book. That is a lifelong task. Rabbi Akiva's story simply illustrates the extent of the achievement that can result from taking that first step. A small amount of effort can have untold consequences, and the opportunity for change is available to everyone.

It is never too late to change.

2. A *tzaddik* is sure that he is capable of great accomplishment. He never has doubts.

In the last chapter (p. 64) we read about Rabbeinu Bachya, the author of the classic *Chovos HaLevavos*. He had many doubts about his writing ability and was about to give up, but fortunately he changed his mind. In listening to a few more of his candid remarks, we may find that they remind us a great deal of ourselves.

> *I suspected myself of seeking relaxation and being lazy. I wanted to have security. I know that many times, things that are within one's potential are lost because of a fear that holds him back from trying; he might fail. If everyone would wait to reach perfection before making an attempt, no person would have spoken (given guidance in Torah) since the period of the prophets. The prophets were chosen by Hashem, and He gave them courage and helped them.*
>
> *If every person who wants to improve would refrain from doing what is within his capability because he wants only to be perfect in everything, then the paths of righteousness would be deserted. No person besides the prophets can reach perfection.*
> (*Chovos HaLevavos, Lev Tov*)

I know it is astounding that this was said 950 years ago by a Torah sage. History has proven to us that the *Sefer Chovos HaLevavos* was a tremendous success, so we assume that Rabbeinu Bachya knew he would succeed before he began. We assume that *gedolim* are aware of their abilities, aware that they are making lasting contributions to the Jewish nation. Rabbeinu Bachya tells us, however, that only a prophet can avoid the pain of self-doubt, because Hashem has told him the future.

One who works on serving Hashem should not become discouraged by self-doubt. He shouldn't feel that his own faults are the cause of an undesirable situation; rather, he should understand that such doubts are part of the human condition. The Bais Yisrael finds a hint to this in the second verse in the Torah: "Don't worry about doubts, because that is the way with all who serve Hashem. At first, *V'haaretz ha'y'sah sohu vavohu* — it seems that the earth is all darkness and confusion. Only after one takes action can the next verse follow: *Vayehi ohr*, the light comes" (*Erchei Chassidus*).

So the answer to the second question is also FALSE.
Those greater than us often doubt their ability to accomplish. Such feelings have little to do with the level that a person has achieved. They have to do with the human condition, and no one is any more or less capable of undertaking new tasks. That includes you!

3. Great men are so good because they only have a good inclination.

In a letter to a student who was lamenting his own spiritual setbacks, Rav Hutner, *zt"l*, deals with this very prevalent misconception:

> *When we consider the perfection of our sages, we focus on the ultimate level of their attainments. We often form the notion that they came out of the hand of their Creator in full-blown form.*

Everyone is awed at the purity of speech of the Chafetz Chaim. But who knows of the battles, struggles, and obstacles, the slumps and regressions that the Chafetz Chaim encountered in his war with the evil inclination?

The result of this (lack of insight) is that when an ambitious young man of spirit and enthusiasm encounters obstacles and stumbles, he imagines himself unworthy of being "planted in the house of Hashem." According to this young man's fancy, flourishing in the house of Hashem means to repose with calm spirit in "lush meadows" beside "tranquil waters" while delighting in the yetzer tov. The righteous delight in the reflection of the Shechinah, in this manner, in Gan Eden.

*My cherished one, I clasp you to my heart and whisper in your ear that had your letter reported on your mitzvos and good deeds, I would have said that I had received a good letter from you. As things stand, with your letter telling of slumps and falls and obstacles, I say that I have received a **very good** letter from you. Your spirit is storming as it aspires to greatness. I beg of you, do not portray for yourself great men as being as one with their yetzer tov. Picture, rather, their greatness in terms of an awesome war with every base and low inclination.*

When you feel the turmoil of the yetzer hara within yourself, know that with that feeling you resemble great men far more than with the feeling of deep peace which you desire. **Particularly** *in those areas where you feel yourself falling most frequently, you have the greatest potential for serving and honoring Hashem.*

(Excerpted from the full letter that appeared in *The Jewish Observer*, December 1981)

Let us review the real truth again:
1. It is never too late to change.
2. Great people do have doubts. They are afraid they won't

reach perfection. But, as Rabbeinu Bachya did, they plunge ahead anyway and do their best.
3. The greatness of a person is in terms of a never-ending war with the *Yetzer Hara*.

If you have ever experienced self-doubt, you are normal. If you have ever felt fearful or hesitant, you are normal. There is no reason to give up on the pursuit of goals and dreams just because of these very common feelings. The hurdles are part of Hashem's plan, and there is a great deal that you can accomplish in spite of them.

Keep reading and you will find out how.

Chapter 6

> There is no despair in the world. Even if it seems that from this failure it is impossible to rise, one cannot know the greatness of Hashem's kindness. Even if, G-d forbid, one failed many times, any action that he makes because he wants to lift himself up, and every cry and scream to G-d, is not lost. One is rewarded for his desire to rise even if afterward he fails again.

(*Halachos, Orach Chaim* page 130; page 426 of *Nesivos HaOsher*)

Recovering From Past Failures

When I was a small child, I broke an expensive glass. I knew my mother would find out. I ran to the living room couch and buried my face in the pillow, reasoning with classic simplicity that if I couldn't see her, she couldn't see me either. It was a lonely feeling, because I knew that she would find me, and the suspense was painful.

Trying to pretend that something unpleasant has not happened, or that if we close our eyes it will disappear, doesn't change the reality. But neither is it healthy to go to the other extreme and carry around guilt for things that are past. The glass incident happened when I was about four years old, but unfortunately, a childlike approach to mishaps is something we often cling to in our adult lives. There is nothing wrong with admitting a mistake and there is nothing wrong with letting go of it and getting on with our lives.

This subject came up during one of the workshops. It seemed that many of the women were carting around vivid memories of past mistakes, and they had labeled themselves failures because of them. They wanted to know how to recover when you realize that you have said the wrong thing; missed your friend's wedding; spilled something on your neighbor's dress. What happens when a family picnic is rained out and it seems to you that you are the only person you know who consistently gets hit with bad weather? What about the cake you spent hours decorating that tastes like cardboard, or the mortgage payment you forgot to mail, or the friend you unintentionally insulted?

In short, what do you do when you feel like a flop?

Failure is Temporary

The first thing to keep in mind is that failure is generally temporary. How many disappointments have you already forgotten? When you keep a perspective on it and realize that this one will fade too, just like the others, it is easier to get back on your feet. Lean on the hope that next time things will go more smoothly and that your pain will be more limited. You *will* succeed in the future.

When you remain hopeful, you will understand mentally that with time the mistake will shrink, even though it feels unpleasant right now. You will be able to look back on it and learn from it because it will no longer seem so crushing.

The Past is No More

The idea that one should not mentally flog himself for past failures can be taken one step further, into the realm of *teshuvah*. We really do not have to waste worry over things that have happened in the past, and we have the ultimate reassurance for this: Hashem Himself has promised us that not only will our failures seem temporary, they will be forgotten altogether.

In the *Foundations of Teshuvah*, Rabbeinu Yonah tells us that the person who wants to return to Hashem should not think to himself: "Why should I pursue this? I'll be working for nothing. My repentance will never succeed because of all the wrong I have done already." He states clearly:

> "Hashem promises that one's sins will not be remembered anymore. In the merit of the good he does from now on, he will live."
> (*Nesivos HaOsher*, by Baruch Reuvain Koenigsburg)

This idea is not specific only to *teshuvah*. It is one that can apply in any area of activity where past mistakes can put a damper on future efforts. We are even told in no uncertain terms that no matter what we have done in the past, we should never view ourselves as inherent failures:

> A person should never see himself as intrinsically bad. The wrong he has done is something that passes, something that can be cleansed and fixed. As G-d said to Avraham, "You said to the guests (the angels who came to visit after Avrohom underwent Bris Milah), 'Let some water be brought and wash your feet.' I promise you that I will repay your children; they will be able to wash their souls."
> The sin is only a covering, but the essence of the person is pure. When the sin is removed, he becomes a new person. (*Yalkut MeAm Lo'ez, Parshas Vayeira*)

There are many other sources which support this train of thought, encouraging us to dissociate ourselves from the unpleasant mistakes of the past when they do not serve any constructive purpose. One of the most famous is the very practical motto of Navardok:

> *The past is no more. The future is not yet. The present is like the blink of an eye. Therefore, why worry?*

Our worry is the tactic of the *Yetzer Hara*. It is a very effective tool for him; when we worry, the damage done by our mistakes is increased because we feel vulnerable. It is worry that makes us want to stay in bed on dreary days and that lets us see only our limitations and not our capabilities.

> *A gang of thieves is planning a robbery. One of the group enters the store, takes some merchandise, and flees. He is hoping that the merchant will chase him and abandon the store, leaving it unguarded so that the rest of his friends can plunder it completely. The smart merchant understands this ploy. He says to himself: "Let the thief keep what he grabbed." He refuses to abandon his post and continues to do business, keeping a careful lookout. He knows that the loss will eventually be recovered, and that he will still earn a profit.*
> (from *Toras Yechezkel*, in *Nesivos HaOsher*)

The merchant in this story kept a clear head and a hopeful outlook. He knew that even though he had lost something, the misfortune was now in the past. He would not be foolish enough to "jump in" after the loss and thereby cause himself more worry and depression. He allowed bygones to be bygones, secure in the knowledge that he could recoup his deficit and continue his endeavors with strength.

This is not just a parable. It is something you can do too.

Hashem Rewards Us for Effort

There is more good news. Not only are past mistakes erased, but we are rewarded for every bit of effort we put in, even when our project does not succeed.

The Chafetz Chaim explains this Divine promise with an analogy to the working world, where the rules do not always accommodate us so well:

> "Well, are my new boots ready?" said the gentleman to the shoemaker.
>
> "I'm sorry, I just couldn't make the boots you ordered, no matter how hard I tried. Here is your bill."
>
> The disappointed customer looked at the piece of paper which the shoemaker handed him. "How can you charge for your labor?" he cried. "You haven't supplied the boots!"
>
> "But I worked for you for several days. So what if I failed to produce the boots you ordered?"
>
> "You don't seem to know the ways of the world. People pay you for results and not for efforts."
>
> At a Siyum Mesechta, we say the following pasuk, which describes the difference between those who engage in Torah study and those who engage in other activities: "They work and we work, but they work without receiving any payment, while we are recompensed for our efforts."
>
> A Jew is secure in the knowledge that he works and receives payment. Even if he has nothing to show for his hours of study, he is rewarded; he is paid for his efforts too. (*Give Us Life*)

The following exercise is an introspective one. It will help you to determine the extent to which your past may be hindering you. In the workshop responses that follow, you will be heartened to discover that a small adjustment in attitude really can work wonders in eliminating the guilt of past mistakes.

Exercise: Getting Rid of the "Baggage"

1. What mistakes have I made that are unpleasant to remember?

   _____

   _____

2. What traits seem to cause me to repeat those mistakes?

   _____

   _____

3. If I could get rid of this baggage of guilt, I would feel free to do these three things:

   a._____

   b._____

   c._____

Chapter 6: Recovering From Past Failures
True Responses

1. I was listening to a tape on raising children. At one point the speaker said, "When your child brings home a report card with a B on it, don't ask him why he didn't do better." I almost passed out; I felt so guilty! That's exactly what I had always said to my own son: "Why didn't you get an A?"

   My son is married now and has three grown children, and I began to realize that my attitude toward him has carried over into other areas. He has put on some weight since he's gotten married, and during every visit I used to comment, "Marvin, when are you going to lose? Why don't you eat less? Why don't you exercise? Why don't you join a swimming class? Why don't you . . . ?"

I decided it wasn't too late to change. When I was there for *Shavuos* this year, I held back on criticism and tried to look for things to compliment. This time I noticed that although he did have cake and blintzes he was trying to be sensible about his eating. I said, "Marvin, I'm so proud of you. I see you're watching what you eat." I can't take back the things I said in the past, but I still have the present. I'm not giving up. I'm using my new awareness as often as I can.

2. I'm a *baalas teshuvah,* and I feel that I've had two life-times. I couldn't just cut myself off from my past. There were things that I had enjoyed and accomplishments that had given me pleasure. Sometimes I would listen to a song on the radio and be reminded of a great party we had had at college.

   One day I was driving to substitute in a Chassidic girls' school. I was wearing a *sheitel* and a long-sleeved dress, and I really looked like I fit the part. But I was listening to the Rolling Stones on the radio! I was in an awful mood for the rest of the day; I felt so guilty and confused. "What's wrong with me?" I kept asking myself. "Who am I?"

   That was a few years ago. Now these things have fallen into perspective. Gradually, as you learn more about Judaism, these things get washed out of your system ... you come to recognize that the lyrics are awful and that the T.V. programs are so full of perverted values. If I had known that this whole thing was a process and that with time I'd change, I wouldn't have had an overactive sense of guilt about these little things from my past.

3. When I hang up the phone and realize there is something I shouldn't have said, I try to talk to Hashem about it right away. I say some *Tehillim* and have in mind: "Hashem, I know it was wrong of me, but You know I meant well and that I didn't intend to hurt anyone or do the wrong thing."

4. I realized that I'd lost contact with three good friends for about a year. Sometimes you're embarrassed to call because the first thing they might ask is why you haven't called until now! I decided to stop feeling guilty for not

keeping in touch and called anyway. The friends were all cheerful and friendly, and didn't blame me. I had agonized for nothing.

5. I have trouble dieting. Once I eat one thing I'm not supposed to, I get so angry at myself that I eat the whole cookie jar. I have to be able to say, "Okay, you're not perfect. Forget the mistake and just be careful from now on."

6. My past came back to haunt me. My married son was going through a difficult time emotionally, and he decided to enter therapy. With these psychologists the mother is always to blame, and sure enough, he called me one day and said, "Mom, you ruined my life because you were overprotective." He said a lot of other things that I can't mention.

My friends advised me to stop talking to him, but that didn't appeal to me. On the other hand, I knew that if I responded to his anger with hostility, the past would haunt us forever, and I even knew some parents who had lost touch with their children that way. I decided to try and let go of the past, and not to become overwhelmed with guilt for mistakes I may have made in his upbringing. I can't say I condoned the way he had approached me, but I subdued my personal hurt and went to see him. All I said was, "You know, David, that I've always loved you, and I always will."
The visit didn't work well and I left quickly, but I continued to keep in touch. He was angry for a good couple of months, but I made an effort to start anew each day and stubbornly remained supportive.

We had some really rough times, but it's completely different now, thank G-d. We are closer than we have ever been, and he has become successful. He's happy with his new job and recently became the father of a baby boy.

Chapter Six □ 83

Chapter 7

> The Chazon Ish once complained to Rabbi Moshe Sheinfeld, "Unfortunately, people usually only bring me their problems. Very few come to tell me their good news — that they have a mazel tov to announce, or that they or their relatives have recovered from illness."

(*Love Your Neighbor* by Zelig Pliskin)

When Things Go Wrong

You have discovered that past mistakes do not have to get in the way of your future. But knowing and feeling don't always go hand in hand.

What happens when things go wrong *now*?

It is so tempting to fall back into our comfortable pattern of negativity. The negative may not be pleasant, but at least it is familiar. It is so easy to let out a sigh and reaffirm our conviction that "nothing ever goes right for me."

On one of his lecture tapes, Rabbi Avigdor Miller explains, "There are two types of success. When things go smoothly, you have succeeded the easy way. But if you can behave gracefully when things have gone wrong, you have truly succeeded."

When people cooperate and are pleasant and considerate; when you are growing and accomplishing; when you receive the ultimate blessing of being appreciated by your beneficiaries that is the easy success.

When people are late, but you keep calm; when something you treasure is lost or broken but you don't scream; when you are insulted and you don't answer back that is *true* success.

There are several techniques to staying on course and keeping your perspective when things go wrong.

Talk To a Positive Person

One thing that works wonders when you are in a muddle is to talk to a person with an upbeat personality. Sometimes a person with a cheerful attitude can help you see the small sparks in the darkness.

One of my friends has ten children, and life in her household is a constant series of ups and downs. Yet Suri's outlook is continually positive. When I ask her how she is doing, she will reply "Oh, today things are fine. Avi had to get stitches yesterday, but he is much better now." Suri sings hello when she answers the phone. When her children answer, they are cheerful too; I guess the spirit of joy is contagious. It is always good to have recourse to happy people.

The "One Good Thing Right Now"

The Chazon Ish's lament was a sad but valid one. We never seem to have any *good* news to tell the rabbi; instead we flood him with our problems. The fact is, we do have "good news" even when things are going wrong, but we have to focus on it.

When you are in a difficult situation, one way to surmount

dejection is to pick out one flower from the pile of rocks. You may have to use your imagination, but the results are well worth the effort.

Kayla had a newborn. He wanted to be carried a lot and ate on a three-hour schedule. He turned day into night and night into day; she was up with him for three weeks in a row. She had five older children, and there was a lot of work to do in the house. She could not rest at all during the day and felt as though she were walking in a fog. Yet she was calm and patient, and managed to handle all the trivialities efficiently. The cherry on top is that she continued to run the school's P.T.A.

"How did you handle everything?" I asked her.

"You know, Roiza," she said, "you always have to look for one good thing right now. One morning I looked out the window and decided that I was up with the baby anyway, so I might as well enjoy the dawn."

Breindy celebrated the *pidyon haben* of her first grandchild about three weeks ago. Her son called her on Friday afternoon to ask if she could send over some food for *Shabbos*. He sounded a little frantic and was worried that the house would not be ready in time for candlelighting; he apparently did not know what it was like to be a new mother! "I don't understand it," he said in frustration. "The house is a mess. It's before *Shabbos*. My wife is always busy but nothing gets done."

"Didn't Leah go to the doctor with the baby yesterday?" Breindy asked her son. "What did he say?"

"Oh, the doctor was very happy. He said the baby is doing fine. He gained very nicely and grew about an inch."

"Well, go tell your wife that she is doing an absolutely wonderful job with the baby. She is a great mother. The baby is thriving," Breindy replied.

When Breindy finished the story, she commented. "Honestly, there are things I don't like about my daughter-in-law, but I think about what I do like instead."

When things go wrong, we have a choice. We can feel

annoyed, or we can decide to see our circumstances differently. We can look for the good in the situation and gain a new perspective on our problem.

Speak Softly

> *Your words should be spoken softly to every person at all times.*   (*Iggeres HaRamban*)

Rabbi Eliyahu Kitov calls our attention to the fact that *Megillas Esther* closes with the ultimate praise of Mordechai: that he "spoke words of peace to his children and grandchildren." Several other attributes are listed first, but the gentle manner in which he approached others underscores his true greatness.

This piece of advice sounds like it belongs in the chapter on interpersonal relationships, but actually it is a very dynamic tactic for handling pressure. Of course, it goes without saying that pleasant words can enhance a relationship, but they also have intrinsic value as a coping mechanism. This idea is beautifully described by Sarah Shapiro in *Growing With My Children:*

"Can this big improvement in the emotional atmosphere be simply the result of a consistent lowering of my voice? Speaking quietly must be affecting my subconscious assessment of life: Since you are not yelling, says my brain, there must be nothing to yell about. I'm coming to the conclusion that life must be okay. Maybe it is even good.

"Staying calm with my children has gotten me into the habit of speaking calmly with my husband, which in turn affects my perception of events. If you are not yelling about it, says my brain, then it is not catastrophic that he forgot to take out the garbage again.

"I'm also not as tired as I usually am. 'Getting all worked up' is an apt expression, because getting angry is hard work."

This Too is For the Best

Mrs. Goodman is a real heroine. She has quietly hosted thousands of guests, helped people with disabilities, and arranged several successful matches.

She says, "When I have put a lot of work into a *shidduch* and it doesn't work out, I say, '*Gam zu l'tovah* — this too is for the best,' and I put some money in the *tzedakah* box. I ask the person I am working with to do it too."

"I understand about saying *Gam zu l'tovah*, but why do you put money in the tzedokah box?" I asked.

"Well," said Mrs. Goodman, "if the shidduch would have been successful, I would have given *tzedakah* to thank Hashem that it worked out, right? So if I really believe that Hashem is in charge and knows what is best, I should give charity when I'm disappointed too."

The concept of *Gam zu l'tovah* was brought home to me in a lecture given last year by Mrs. Chaia Erblich, director of the Shalheves program in Monsey. At the time it sounded a bit too ideal for me.

"It is possible to turn everyday experiences into plain, simple bliss," she had emphasized. "Experiences like taking a walk with the baby, cooking for *Shabbos,* losing your temper, getting into an argument and then having the courage to say, 'I'm sorry,' first ... even having hot oil splatter on your forehead. Well, of course you are not going to splatter oil on your forehead on purpose. But once you've already done it, it is a debt paid. When you pay off money that you owe, do you feel bad about not having the money anymore? It might hurt a little, but it feels so marvelous to be free."

About three months ago, Chaia herself was driving and was hit by another car. Her children emerged from the impact without a scratch, but Chaia was confined to bed for about three months. She was discussing the experience with her ten-year-old daughter and asked out of curiosity, "Shani, what did I say when the car hit us, before I passed out?" Shani answered, "Mommy, you said, '*Gam zu l'tovah.*'"

When I had first heard this *shiur*, I said to myself, "Not me!" I worry a lot; I'm more serious, not the "happy-go-lucky" type. I really become unglued when I'm tired and under pressure. While I was listening, a part of me was remembering a Thursday in the country the summer before.

While adding something to a hot frying pan, the oil had splattered and burnt my hand. At first I thought it wasn't too bad. I ran cold water over it and that camouflaged the pain, so I went about with my other tasks and tried to forget the burn. But I couldn't. The pain kept coming back; it burned and burned and burned. The hand began to worry me, and I became frantic. I took out all the remedies in my medicine chest a spray, a cream, a powder but nothing really worked.

From the moment I left that lecture, I had begun saying *Gam zu l'tovah*, even though I didn't have much confidence in the outcome. I said it even when I had just had an outburst of anger. I was constantly challenging myself, wondering if it would ever become an automatic reaction. It had seemed like an impossible dream.

Then, on a recent Friday afternoon, the cooking accident reoccurred. I was in the midst of putting up my *Yerushalmi kugel* when the boiling hot water spilled on me. It was almost a year since I had heard that *shiur*, but the first words to pop out of my mouth were "*Gam zu l'tovah*" even before I shouted, "Oh, no!" I had found something to alleviate the pain that really worked; I was able to experience joy at being burned instead of screaming and feeling awful. The realization that I had grown overshadowed the sensation of heat on my wrist. When I looked in the mirror, my skin was all red, yet I didn't feel the pain.

In the *sefer Cheshbon HaNefesh*, Rav Yehuda Lieb Zabarz describes two ways to conquer the spiritual enemy. One can attack with all one's strength and catch him by surprise, or one can use wisdom to bring the enemy gradually to agree with him. With the first method you achieve your goal quickly, but you use up a lot of strength. The second way preserves strength but takes time.

This is why, in earlier generations, when people were strong and able to generate fear of Hashem to overcome the *Yetzer Hara*, the first method was preferred. It is said about Moshe Rabbeinu that even fear of Hashem was easy for him. Today we do not have that strength, but we can still change by taking an easy step and repeating it persistently without giving up. As it says in *Iyov* (14:19), "The water broke the rock."

It had taken me over a year to turn a forced, mechanical reaction into a part of my nature. It still requires a bit of effort, but the dividends are tremendous.

Here is something else you may find interesting: A positive attitude is not just a psychological phenomenon, it has physiological roots as well. Research has determined that when a person feels cheerful, his system generates hormones called endorphins, which are natural pain-blockers. Somehow this doesn't seem surprising; our *chachamim* knew the answers years ago, way in advance of modern medicine.

You now have several functional strategies for making the best out of an unpleasant situation. Let us review them:

1. Talk to a positive person.
2. Find the "one good thing right now."
3. Speak softly.
4. Say, "*Gam zu l'tovah*."
5. Put some money in the *tzedakah* box.
6. Call your rabbi with some good news!

This chapter was full of practical tips, so we are not going to do an exercise this time. You deserve a break. Take the afternoon off and do something nice for yourself.

Chapter 8

> *When you are walking in narrow places, such as on the top of a wall that surrounds a city, Hashem will help you to walk with confidence, without slipping.*
>
> (*Ibn Ezra* on *Tehillim*, 121:3)

Anxiety About the Future: The Un-panic Button

"Whenever I work very hard on something, my stomach hurts because I'm afraid that something beyond my control will happen to ruin it."

"If I am involved in planning or coordinating a major event, I worry until the last minute. Will enough people come? Will the sound system hold up? Will the food be good?"

"For two years I have been working for a certain

charity, but I never went to the meetings; I was afraid to participate in a group. When someone asks me for an opinion, I'm afraid I'll say something stupid, or that people might take advantage of me. What if they write me down for a job I don't like? I won't be able to say no."

"I've been sewing for a long time, yet even now, when I see a complicated pattern, I feel this sudden loss of confidence. I'm afraid to make a mistake."

"I had to go apologize to a neighbor. I knew I must apologize. I couldn't take the lack of shalom, that cold look you see in the other person's eyes when he passes you in the street. But my heart was in my hands."

Do any of these remarks sound familiar? Chances are you have said one or more of them in your adult life. Anxiety about the unknown is one of the chief roadblocks to achievement, and it hits most people on various levels.

When I was seven, my mother sent me to the grocery store around the corner. She tucked a short shopping list and a five-dollar bill into my small red pocketbook, brought me a sweater, and watched from the doorway as I crossed the street. I skipped down the sidewalk, but when I reached the corner I hesitated. My house suddenly seemed too far away. Just for a moment I panicked, but the heady sense of independence that I was experiencing won out, and I continued on my way. There were a number of people on line in the grocery store and some of them were pushing, but I did manage to speak up and request my purchases. I handed the clerk my money, and he gave me the change. As soon as I got home, I called my grandmother, my aunt, and my big sister to share my exciting adventure with them. I had gone to the grocery store by myself and what fun it had been!

It is interesting to think back to childhood when we talk about fear of the unknown. Somehow it seems that young children are less afraid of "hazards" than we are. They do not have an entire litany in their heads of things that could possibly go wrong. We rode a bicycle when we were young but we might be afraid to get on one now. We rode the roller coaster at the amusement park and had a wonderful time, but we are petrified to watch our own kids do the same thing!

Why is it that as adults we somehow lose our nerve?

Perhaps we feel we are more fragile now. In the back doors of our minds, there are a variety of wonderful projects that we could accomplish. If we were to honestly evaluate our abilities, we would conclude that we could make it happen. What is the mysterious barrier that compels us to shut the door quickly and become defensive of the status quo? Concentrating on past mistakes certainly impedes progress, but too much worry about the future can block the road completely.

This type of worry is not only unhealthy for us, it affects others too. When we are busy with a project, we put ourselves and everyone around us under extraordinary pressure. There are a million questions that haunt us at every hour, logical and illogical, and our desperate desire to have everything perfect backfires on our family and friends.

Debby told me, "I made a *Sheva Brachos* for a relative last fall. This year I wanted to do it again for a different relative, but my husband wasn't too supportive. His reason surprised me: 'I don't mind the work or the expense, I mind the tension! You were so nervous and jumpy the last time you did this that we couldn't talk to you all week.'"

Our *chachamim* are well aware of the adverse effects of anxiety. Rabbi Moshe Chaim Luzzatto says that trepidation cools off our enthusiasm for *mitzvos*. He lists a number of things that one might be afraid of: An accident might happen; we might get sick; there could be bad weather.

But the *chachamim* have also provided a clear antidote an "un-panic button" that is accessible and that we can use any time:

> Trust in Hashem and you will have strength to do good. As it says in Tehillim (37:3): *"Trust in G-d and do good."* (Mesilas Yeshorim)

This is not simply an instruction to do good. It is an indication that trusting in Hashem will actually give us the ability to do good and to succeed in any area of life.

In *Tehillim* (121:3), Dovid *HaMelech* declares:

"Hashem will not allow your foot to falter." Radak explains that these are the words of encouragement with which the Jewish people in exile will strengthen each other all through the ages. He says that we will do well to place our faith in Hashem, for He will not fail us; He will help us to take firm steps and will prevent us from falling.

Reb Meir of Premishlan would climb a steep mountain every morning of the year in order to immerse in the natural *mikveh* that was at the peak. The snow and ice that covered the mountain did not chill Reb Meir's determination.

One snowy morning some troublemakers decided to climb the mountain, planning to entertain themselves at the *Rebbe's* expense. Reb Meir began his ascent and the ruffians followed. During the climb they slipped and fell several hundred feet, suffering severe injuries.

"How does he do it?" they wondered. "We are young and keep ourselves fit, but on our first attempt we fell. How does the old man climb that mountain every day?" They approached the *Rebbe* and begged forgiveness, realizing that there must be something special about him. "How do you climb that mountain every day without slipping?" they asked.

Reb Meir answered: **"When one is bound to the ABOVE, he doesn't fall below."**

What is the "un-panic button" for those apprehensive moments when you feel you cannot go on?

The antidote to fear is faith. Attachment to the Above is what keeps us from slipping.

Having faith in the face of the unknown seems like an undertaking too big to conquer, but it is not. A little prayer can get you started. Put your finger on the page of a *sefer* or a *siddur*. Don't say, "I have no patience to learn or to pray." When you pick up a *siddur*, the *siddur* picks you up.

On the following pages there are some more specific *bitachon* exercises that you can practice to put yourself in a calmer frame of mind when you are worried about a task or decision that faces you.

Exercise Chapter 8: Bitachon Basics

The following small mental exercises are culled from a truly wonderful *sefer* called *Sefer Mitzvas HaBitachon*, by Rabbi Shmuel Huminer. One of the women in the workshop recommended it to me, explaining that this *sefer* has an invisible strength and that learning from it consistently can increase one's peace of mind.

This kind of guarantee was not one to be taken lightly! I ran out and bought it the next day, and I try to keep it with me always. It is so small, yet it contains so much. The first chapter is a collection of Torah verses. The Maharal says that the recitation of these verses will protect one from danger and ensure success. The second section contains short anecdotes and lessons in faith, gathered from many early sources.

The following excerpts from the *sefer* are a special source of strength for me. Please do not think of them as a demand for you to "work on your faith." Such global tasks are doomed to failure by the very nature of their size. No one can improve his faith overnight. Rather, these verses contain thoughts and suggestions which are calming and comforting. You can repeat the ideas to yourself, or even say the *pesukim* quietly whenever you are worried about the future. They really do work.

Tefillah is for everything you need.

Pray to Hashem. Pour out your heart to Him every day, at any time and at any moment. Ask for small

> *needs and large needs. Trust in Hashem to help you with problems and to prepare the way for you (p. 1).*

Our problems do not have to become dire before we seek Hashem's help. He is there all day long, for the small things too. You can *daven* for something as "unimportant" as finding a lost item or getting to a certain place on time. Hashem does not discriminate. He doesn't consider our worries too trivial.

Bitachon gets you free kindness.

> *In Tehillim (32:10) it says, "One who trusts in the Almighty will be surrounded by kindness." Even if a person is not worthy, faith will draw free kindness for those who trust in G-d (p. 48).*

When I was four, I filled out one of my father's checks for a thousand dollars and gave it to him for a birthday present. My father laughed and said, "You can't write checks if you don't have money in the bank." This holds true for money but fortunately, not for faith! When we pray, we can write "checks" even if there isn't any "money" in the account.

Rely on Hashem's kindness.

> *Depend on Hashem. It is best when one relies on Hashem's free kindness. However, one is not always sure that this will be effective; since he assumes he isn't worthy of free kindness, he doesn't honestly count on his prayers. That is why the request isn't granted. If he would honestly trust in G-d, G-d would not withhold His kindness. G-d always wants to give blessing to one who honestly trusts in Him (p. 48).*

Anxiety creates problems.

> *Anxiety creates problems. It strengthens the enemy and brings anguish. Yet faith will protect one even from harm that was supposed to come to him (p. 68).*

Lock your door but rely on Hashem.

> *Two people do the same deed. One locks his door or runs to the shelter and relies on it. He is pitiful and will be punished. The other one relies on Hashem. He locks his door or runs to the shelter and prays to Hashem for success. He is fortunate; Hashem will reward his trust and help him and save him. Understand this deeply. Remember it constantly* (p. 88).

This excerpt is important because it reminds us that we do have to take physical measures to insure our safety. The difference is in our attitude. If we acknowledge where our *real* security is coming from, we will be better protected by the physical measures we take to protect us.

Don't be afraid of people.

> *No person can help or cause harm unless Hashem allows it. Trust only in Him* (p. 128).

Chapter 9

> Imagine that you purchased this vacant lot, erected a house here, and lived here for thirty years. Then one night the telephone rings, and you hear a quavering old voice: "I must inform you that I am the last survivor of a group that buried a chest of gems on the premises where your house now stands. I am about to die, and therefore I wish you to know." Now you are so delirious with joy that you cannot sleep. You are wealthy! But actually for thirty years you were the legal possessor of the unclaimed treasure. What is the factor which makes you happy today instead of thirty years earlier?
>
> It is the knowledge of what we possess. If we are unaware of what we have, or only faintly aware of its true value, we actually do not possess it.

(*Sing, You Righteous*, Rabbi Avigdor Miller)

The Impossible Dream

Up to this point we have been discussing various ways to break down the mental obstacles that inhibit growth. The exercises are helpful, but the real key to growth is the understanding that we don't need outside factors to give us a sense of self-worth and the confidence to approach new ventures. The secret is within us: It is the knowledge that all along we have been the owners of an unused treasure.

It is not difficult to open the chest and enjoy that treasure. You are already holding the key.

In that treasure chest of your personality and history, there are successes. You have already accomplished things that are worthy of note, things that reflect on your worth as a person. You may have created an excellent project in school, knitted a sweater, gotten someone a job, or listened patiently when a friend was in trouble. The event may have seemed "impossible" at the time, and yet you succeeded. But for various reasons you have allowed the memory of those deeds to atrophy.

Sometimes we don't like to be reminded that we actually have abilities, because then we might be challenged to use them. We think that holding back gives us peace of mind, but in truth, when we are understimulated and disorganized, we feel empty. As Rav Yitzchak Greenberg (a well-known Rav in Petach Tikva) said, "Most people use only about fifteen percent of their inner resources. They lock up the rest in a chest and mark it: Do not open."

Another reason we might resist peering inside the chest is because others may have convinced us it is not worth opening.

I have been privileged to teach several adults to read *sefarim* in the original Hebrew. These were women with no background, yet after a year of studying once a week for an hour and a half, they made tremendous progress. Some of them were able to read better than a Bais Yaakov graduate. I thought that perhaps the first person I taught was simply a genius. But after seeing the same results with several others students, I began to think it was something else: These women had a clean slate with regard to this particular skill. They had never studied it in school, so they had never gone through the process of criticism in Hebrew reading. No teacher had ever embarrassed them or made them feel weak in this area, so they had no reason to think they could not do it. They pursued it consistently and were rewarded with success.

Perhaps when you were a child, a teacher or peer told you that you could not do a particular thing well. You were not picked for the choir or you were not picked for dance. Afterward you gave up on those very things.

You are assuming that because it was hard then, it must be hard now. Your thoughts probably run something like this: "Others can do it better. I'm not really good at anything. My sister is the genius in the family; I'm the *klutz.*"

We think it is righteous to put ourselves down, and in the process we subdue the memory of our past successes, dismissing them as "just lucky." What we don't realize is that it takes a lot of strength and determination to quash a good memory, but when it serves our purposes we are able to do it. If we are that strong, we can channel our determination in the opposite direction as well.

Rav Eliyahu Lopian makes this point unequivocally: "We must accept our accomplishments. Make sure to remember your triumphs, because they will help you to serve Hashem." He illustrates this concept with the following story.

The Lion-Skin Jacket

> When Dovid was a shepherd, a fierce lion and a wild bear attacked the sheep. Dovid battled against the lion and the bear simultaneously. He tore them apart with his bare hands.
>
> "I could not have conquered even a lion. Yet now both the lion and the bear lie dead at my feet. It is a sign from Hashem: Sometime in the future I will have to defend Bnei Yisrael. I need not fear because Hashem will help me."
>
> Dovid made a jacket from the lion's skin, which he wore from that time on, to remind him constantly of his miraculous triumph and its portent for the future.
>
> Several years later, war broke out. For forty days the giant, Goliath the Plishti, stood up and faced the Jewish camp. He cursed Hashem and said, "You Jews are cowards. Your G-d cannot help you against me. I am a mighty giant. Send a representative to fight me. If he wins, we will serve you, but if I win, all of you Jews will become our slaves."

None dared to challenge him. Then Dovid came to the battlefield. He heard of the challenge and said, "I will fight Goliath." The people laughed, but Dovid went to King Shaul.

"You are young and small and inexperienced at war," King Shaul said to him. "His head reaches the clouds! How will you conquer that giant? Our nation's future depends on this."

Dovid showed his lion-skin jacket and replied, "Hashem who saved me from the lion and the bear will save me from this Philistine."

The strong weight of habit is a lion that dwells within us. We must conquer it with our bare hands. Make an effort to recall your triumphs, and thank Hashem for helping you to overcome your desires. By savoring those times when you pulled through, you will generate the courage to say, "Somehow I'll handle this one too."

I asked the women in the workshop for stories of their own "impossible deeds," and I think you will find the following one very inspirational.

Yael's Story

When I asked Yael if she could remember doing something "impossible," something that really made her feel like a winner, her first reaction was negative.

"You want to know when I've felt confident? I can't remember anything. . . Oh, one minute, there *is* something you might want to hear about. Yes, this is good. You can't imagine how incredible I felt when this happened.

"About seven years ago, I passed a store. I went in to buy some socks, but I found myself in the middle of a heated discussion. The woman behind the counter was trying to convince a customer to get rid of her television. I laughed and said to the owner, 'Don't worry, dear, I have one too,' as though to indicate that it was not such a terrible thing.

"She looked at me, her eyes wide open in surprise. 'You too?' she said. 'You have that destructive force in your home?'

"I'm not the type to get insulted. I figured she can have her way and I can have mine. I paid for the socks and left but her words stayed in my mind. 'Destructive Force. Destructive Force.' Those words stuck in my head. I continued to watch television because it was very entertaining, but sometimes when the children walked in, I'd feel guilty. I would see those words 'Destructive Force' in big letters in front of me.

"Then I went to a gathering on the Tenth of Teves. The *gedolim* who spoke to us were crying . . . *gedolim* were crying. Those honest Jewish tears did something to me. When I came home I saw the television, and it really bothered me.

"I took it out and put it in the garbage. My friend, my comforting companion in times of stress I just got rid of it in a minute. Roiza, I felt like such a winner. You can't imagine how incredible it felt.

"I thought of changing my mind; I missed it. I looked out the window and I could see it there on top of the garbage a Sony 19" color T.V. I felt so free, as though I had just been released from a prison."

Yael's story is an illustration of the verse in *Mishlei* which says: תַּאֲוָה נִהְיָה תֶּעֱרַב לְנָפֶשׁ, "When one can break a desire that is ruling over him, there is a wonderfully pleasant feeling in his soul" (*Mishlei* 13:19).

Yael told me that many times since then, when she is at a point of crisis, she thinks of that winter afternoon on *Asarah B'Teves*. When she remembers her triumph, she finds the conviction to handle the obstacles presently before her.

We have more strength than we know we possess. All we have to do is open up the treasure chest and remember our achievements, however small they may seem and then we have to *continue* to remember, wearing our successes like a lion-skin jacket.

Exercise Chapter 9: The Lion-Skin Jacket

1. Go back into your memory and pull out one single "impossible" deed that you attempted and completed successfully, even though the outcome may have surprised you. You may want to write about something that you did last year, or perhaps you will go further back into your past to recall an incident from your childhood. Concentrate. Choose something that really made you feel like a winner.

    The act of writing down your positive memory is your creation of a personal "lion-skin jacket." You can review it when you feel low, and draw new conclusions about what you can probably do well right now.

    _____
    _____
    _____
    _____
    _____
    _____

2. What was unique and new about this experience?

    _____
    _____

3. What special talent or inner strength did you discover?

    _____
    _____

4. The visual image of an encouraging face can enhance the effect of an event. Picture yourself telling one of your

favorite people about your achievement and record the imaginary conversation.

_____

_____

_____

_____

_____

Chapter 9: The "Impossible" Deed True Responses

1. I went to a *teshuvah* rally during the Ten Days of Repentance, and the speaker spoke against the typical *Chol Hamoed* outings that most families go on, saying that they took away from the holiday's holiness. He advised us to spend more time with our children in the *succah* itself. As I listened I wondered, "Is it possible to keep my five children at home and preserve the holiday spirit? What if I have chaos?"

   I discovered an eleven-year-old girl who is talented at arts and crafts. She came to our house, took the children into the *succah,* and helped them create a very original booklet about the seven days of creation. The children had a marvelous time, cutting, pasting, and using glitter, and I felt much calmer than in previous years, when we had spent the days running around.

2. I feel very uneasy about calling and asking for money, even if it's for a good cause. In the past five years I've been asked dozens of times to make fundraising calls, and I've simply refused. This time, though, I couldn't say no because the person who asked needed money to marry off her daughter, and I knew the situation was serious.

   I made a few calls and got several people to agree to send

in eighteen dollars. The last person I called said, "I'll drop it off at your house," but she never came. About a month later I saw an envelope at my door marked, "Poor Brides Fund," and inside was fifty dollars. I learned two things from this episode that I can ask for money if I have to, and that we should always give people the benefit of the doubt!
3. I'm a divorcee with three children, and I lived in Virginia until a month ago. This past winter I met a man who lives in Brooklyn. In February I came to Brooklyn with my children because it really looked like we'd get married. I began making plans to move here; I rented an apartment and found a job for the coming summer.

    Then my plans began to erode. This man decided that we weren't right for each other, and the office where I had gotten a job decided not to hire me. I took my life in my hands and decided to move here anyway because the community is so vibrant, and I knew my children would get a better Jewish education. When I boarded the plane I had no idea what I would do, but within a week I had a job.
4. My impossible deed is getting up in the morning! You really need to be strong for that one. The *Yetzer Hara* is always telling me that I need more sleep.
5. I'm thinking of when my children were born. That was really the biggest accomplishment of my life. All of a sudden there is this little person next to you. Wow! You feel a light go on inside you that is so bright!
6. Last year I was a dorm counselor at a school for *baalos teshuvah* in Israel. Dealing with the girls is always very sensitive, and you have to be careful with your words, because you don't know who will remain religious and who will turn away. One girl came to talk to me night after night. Her situation was very rough, and at one point she said, "I'm at the end of the rope. Why should I continue? I have no friends."

    We talked her problems over all night and reviewed everything we had discussed during the previous nights. That was a year ago; just last week she called and told me that she had found a job and was doing outreach work with NCSY. She was on her way to a friend's house for *Shabbos*. I felt a tremendous sense of gratification.

7. I remember the time I invited a Russian family to our *succah*. It was their first meal in a *succah*. They walked in and gazed at the walls and at the ceiling. They were like young children who had entered a fairyland. In this special world they laughed and relaxed. In the half year that I had known them, I had never seen this family really enjoy a visit so much. It felt wonderful; I had given them a "first" in their lives.

8. I became religious. That was quite an impossible deed!

9. I am a social worker, and I remember the time I convinced a family to accept the child who had just been born to them with a birth defect. Many people think that social workers are good at this kind of thing after all, isn't that what we were trained for? However they don't see the dozens of cases that end in failure, despite our best efforts. Sometimes the situation is beyond our control.

    This mother was very depressed and did *not* want to take her child. I worked for eight months to get that baby home, talking to her and working with the older siblings. Today the child sits in a regular classroom. You cannot imagine the feeling of accomplishment. Sometimes the "impossible deed" is really a miracle.

Chapter 10

> *Know that a person is influenced through his actions. His heart and thoughts follow the things he is busy with.*
>
> (Rav Aharon Halevi, *Sefer Hachinuch*)

The Motivation to Grow

In *Tehillim* (24:3), Dovid *HaMelech* poses the challenging question, מִי יַעֲלֶה בְהַר ה׳ וּמִי יָקוּם בִּמְקוֹם קָדְשׁוֹ, "Who can climb up Hashem's mountain, and *continue* to stay in His holy place?"

We work so hard to attain a lofty feeling, but our motivation flies away from us. How can we retain it long enough to accomplish something? Up until now we have been talking mainly about psychological barriers to growth but now it is time to act.

One day I was sitting in the subway train, and I glanced around at some of the advertisements in the car. I was surprised at how many different products and services were offered in just this one car. One could send his children to camp, go to college, buy a kitchen, or get phone service. Anyone worried about his health had two dentists and two surgeons to choose from.

About five minutes later I suddenly realized that all these different advertisements had something in common an 800 number. Most of the numbers were catchy: 1-800-DENTIST, 1-800-244-LASER, 1-800-DAY CAMP, or 1-800-KITCHEN. I counted ten 800 numbers altogether.

The services sold in these notices are not cheap. Surely if one is considering a new kitchen or laser surgery, he can afford to make one phone call. Why is that first phone call free? Does it really influence a person to buy?

An 800 line is an expensive investment for a firm, yet they are so popular that there is a separate directory and a special operator for them. These businesses know that once you take that first step, there is a probability that you will eventually go all the way. So they make the first step easy for you. "Just make the start and call today," these advertisements shout.

There is a great deal of wisdom in this tactic and it is not restricted to business. In fact, taking the first step is the very key to sustaining the motivation that seems so elusive.

You have to ask yourself, "What can I change TODAY?" You have to take something new upon yourself, even if it is only very slight. Perhaps it is the decision to make a *Sheva Brachos* even though you aren't in the mood, to take a guest for *Shabbos,* or to bake *challah* even though your mother never did it. You build one success on another. When the next challenge comes up, you will be able to say to yourself, "If last week I was able to do _____ then maybe now I can even do _____."

Rav Aharon Halevi tells us in *Sefer HaChinuch* that actions have the power to change our characters:

Through our actions, noble feelings will be implanted in our hearts forever.

> *My son, do not think you can catch me on this and say, "But why did G-d command so many intricate practices in order for us to remember the Exodus? Wouldn't one mitzvah have been enough for a commemoration?"*
>
> *Know, my son, that your question does not come from wisdom but from the inexperience of youth. Listen closely, and I will teach you the secret of success in Torah and mitzvos. Know that a person is influenced through his actions. His heart and thoughts follow the things he is busy with.*
>
> *If a completely evil person will wake up and begin investing effort in Torah and mitzvos, even though his motives aren't pure, he will turn to good. The power of action will kill the Yetzer Hara. One's heart follows after one's deeds.*
>
> *A completely righteous person with a straight and upright heart may want Torah. Yet if he becomes occupied with hurtful deeds, albeit against his will — if the government, for example, forces him to become a tax collector he will eventually become an evil person. Because one's heart follows after one's deeds.*

The important revelation in this passage is that deeds are not dependent on feelings in fact, quite the contrary. If you wait to be in the "right mood" to start your project, you will never start. Everything hinges on the first move you make however slight, however uneven, however doubtful it is.

We all get stuck in the "tomorrow syndrome." The *Yetzer Hara* cannot tell us, "Don't do the *mitzvah*," because that would be a foolhardy attack. He knows we are well aware of right and wrong. So instead he takes the devious route, coaxing us to wait a little longer.

I had planned to say *Krias Shema* from a *siddur* each night. One night at 12:30, when I was about to drop off to sleep, I was suddenly reminded of my plan. But I was so tired; the bed was very comfortable. It wouldn't be so bad, I thought, if I didn't use a *siddur* for one more day. Tomorrow I would surely remember.

Diets begin "tomorrow." The letter we have to write will be sent "tomorrow"...

The Rebbe of Slonim says that it is hard for us to awaken our awareness of Hashem and to activate our potential today because the *Yetzer Hara* argues, "Wait for tomorrow. Tomorrow it is fine to obey Hashem, but today listen to me." We should fight him with his own strategy: "Listen, today I'm going to do the right thing, and tomorrow we'll talk about it."

I once visited someone in Jerusalem who had really mastered this principle, Rebbetzin Esther Segal. She told me that she wakes up at two A.M. every morning to do bookkeeping and write letters. When I asked her how she did it, she replied, "First I get out of bed, and then I ask Hashem for help. You can't pray for help while you are still inert; you have to make an effort first."

Preparing a Vessel

Hashem promises us that He will make our ideals a reality if we only try and are persistent. There are many examples in Torah and *Navi* of people who attempted the "impossible." They had no idea if they would succeed, but they took a leap of faith and made that slight first move. G-d rewarded their sincerity.

The prophet Ovadiah's widow once came crying to Elisha for help (*II Kings* 4:1-7). "You know that my husband spent a fortune to hide and sustain one hundred prophets from the wicked Queen Izevel, who wanted to murder them. When our fortune was spent, he borrowed from Yehoram, Achav and Izevel's son. Yehoram has come to me now to demand payment. He wants me to give my sons to him as servants since we are poor and cannot repay the loan. Save my deceased husband's honor," the widow pleaded. "Save my sons. If Prince Yehoram takes them, he will raise them to worship idols."

"What do you have of value in the house?" asked Elisha.

"I have nothing except a small amount of oil, enough for one smearing," replied the widow. This expensive oil was scented with the rare herb *afarsimon*, and was used as a perfume.

Elisha told her to prepare as many pots, pans, and other vessels as she had on hand, and to borrow additional ones from the neighbors. Then he instructed her to close the door and begin pouring the small drop of oil that she had left.

A miracle occurred. The oil poured and poured; it did not stop. Finally her sons shouted, "There are no more whole vessels." She said, "Bring the broken ones. If G-d wills it, they too can hold oil." When there were not any containers left, the oil became a fountain in her home.

Elisha had told the widow to prepare the empty containers even though she did not yet have anything to fill them with.

Rav Yechezkel Sarna, *zt"l,* questions this advice, pointing out that the widow technically did not have to prepare the pots. If Hashem wanted to make a miracle, He could just as easily have caused the pots to appear too. He explains: The widow had to take this preliminary step. She had to begin and show that she believed, although she couldn't visualize the results of the action. What would these empty vessels be filled with? She had nothing.

Likewise, we ourselves are to become a vessel. If we prepare ourselves, Hashem will fill our lives with blessing. We can feel in our hearts what our effort must be. *We should not procrastinate.* The more we strive, the more fulfilled our lives will become (*Gevuras Yitzchak*).

> *The menorah that we light on Chanukah is a beautiful demonstration of this principle. On the first night we light only one candle, and there are seven empty cups. Each night those cups are gradually filled. They represent the idea that vessels have to be prepared even if we are not ready to fill them right now.*
>
> *Strive to have goals prepared. You may not be able to fulfill them now, but you must yearn. Each day you*

> will light one more "cup." You will take another small step closer to Hashem.   (*Insights*, Rabbi Berel Bell)

You do not have to be concerned about the outcome. You only have to be on the way. In the Torah itself is a promise that the things requested of us in life are not beyond our reach. They are in our mouths and in our hearts.

The treasure is within us. We only have to take the first small step. Here is an exercise that will help you get started.

Exercise Chapter 10: Taking the First Step

For this exercise you will need a cup filled with any drink except grape juice. You will also need a few quiet moments and the decision to be open minded about a familiar experience.

> *Rav Gedaliah Schorr zt"l said to me, "You know the Sadigerer Rebbe was niftar two nights ago. I spoke with someone who was at his bedside on the night of his passing. He said that the Rebbe awoke in the middle of the night and asked for a drink of water. He said the brachah, Shehakol Nehiyeh Bedivaro. After that he fell asleep again and passed away during the night.*
>
> *Our sages tell us that one who lives his entire life with a firm belief in Hashem will merit that his last words will testify to just that. Shehakol Nehiyeh Bedivaro — All exists according to the word of G-d." The Rosh Yeshivah paused for a moment, then smiled and waved goodbye. Those were his last words to me.*
> (Biography of Harav Gedaliah Schorr by Rabbi Nosson Scherman; *The Jewish Observer* 1979)

How many *brachos* do we say each day? Yet we never realize the power in that act. A *brachah* can affect our entire future if we say it with heart. You do not have to go far. You can begin to mine the magic right now. Put this book down and dedicate a few moments to Hashem by making a *brachah* over your drink and really say it with heart.

How did you feel when you made that *brachah*?

_____

_____

You have just taken an important first step, and that is only the beginning. Remember that a small act of devotion to Hashem has a ripple effect. *Chazal* tell us: "*Mitzvah goreres mitzvah.*" If we begin on the right track, Hashem will activate a strong magnetic force to help us continue. Even a tiny bit of progress will propel us forward.

> *For each action that a person does, a spirit is given to him from above. This spirit has no rest until the person performs this type of action again.*
>
> (Vilna Gaon, *Even Shelaima*)

We are talking about positive *actions*, not positive *feelings*. Remember that if you wait until you feel motivated, you may never act. The *Sefer HaChinuch*'s secret is a potent one:

Motivation Comes From Doing.

Chapter 10: The Motivation To Grow
True Responses

In this workshop, the women gave examples of "wobbly" first steps they had taken in different areas of endeavor. Their efforts did not always work out the first time around, but the knowledge that they had taken action gave them the strength to continue.

1. I have had a fear of medical things ever since I was a small child. I remembering becoming hysterical in kindergarten because a girl broke her arm and came to school in a cast. I couldn't look at it and begged the teacher to let me go home. Even when I became older, the sight of an amputee or of people wearing bandages would give me horrible

nightmares for days afterward. The idea of going into a nursing home was not even a notion that I could entertain mentally. But at the same time it bothered me that I could not overcome these fears and do that type of *chessed*.

When I was in seminary, the nursing home near our school went on strike, and all the girls took shifts to help out. I stayed in the dormitory and cried. I just could not force myself to go into that building, but I felt so guilty; I thought I must not be a kind person inside.

About three years later I suddenly decided that I wasn't going to tolerate this nonsense any longer. There was a nursing home near my apartment, and before I lost my nerve, I called up a friend and asked her to come with me. I felt nauseated, but I went in.

The smell was overwhelming. The people were lined up in their wheelchairs on both sides of the hallway with their hands outstretched, begging to be touched. I was completely flustered. I went up and down the hallway and said hello to as many people as I could, but after about half an hour my stamina gave out.

It's been ten years, and I still go to the nursing home every week.

2. I had just moved to a new city and didn't know anyone. I felt so shy and uncomfortable. I'd walk out with my children on the avenue and feel totally alone. I didn't have the courage to introduce myself to anyone.

The *rebbetzin* of our *shul* is very friendly. She came over to me and didn't wait for me to say hello first. I'd been living here for a few months when she saw me at the grocery store and said, "We want to hold a meeting for the women, and Mrs. Schwarz offered her home. Could you perhaps make a fruit platter?"

I was so surprised. I was also very nervous because there is something in me that will not let me do things in the ordinary way. That day I was at the library taking out books on how to make food arrangements. I had always been good at art and these books captivated me. I practiced the procedures for hours. At times I'd get frustrated because it still wasn't working out right. I lacked the patience to follow the steps.

Believe it or not, my husband explained what I had to do when I was stuck. I had been trying to copy the pictures instinctively, but he is very detail oriented and guided me patiently. I've done much better work since then, but even my first attempt was beautiful. That fruit platter introduced me to all the women of our *shul*. Since then I've even done fruit sculpture professionally.

3. A while back I decided I would begin saying *Tehillim* every day. On the first day I woke up at 6:00 A.M. to do it. I am not a morning person, and I really feel pretty sick at that hour, but this was the only way I could manage; my kids get up soon afterward and the mornings in my house are impossibly hectic. I kept that up for a week and had a relapse, but the wonderful feeling of saying *Tehillim* to Hashem had given me such a sense of inner tranquility that I decided I just couldn't give it up so easily. Those were my quiet moments to speak to Hashem, and it was worth the discomfort.

After another two weeks, I woke up again, and this time I didn't have quite as bad a resistance to the hour. Now I don't wake up quite that early, but the routine has become part of my life. If I can't do it in the morning, I try to do it in five-minute segments sometime during the day. It is already two years, and thank G-d, I'm keeping it up.

4. When I was still in seminary, we had a very dynamic guest speaker. His theme was one that unfortunately has become very popular — the fact that the media affects us on a subconscious level. I wondered, "What would he think if he knew I went to movies?" I decided then to give up going to the movies.

I'm not sure you understand the difficulties this entailed. Since my family customarily went to a movie every *Motza'ei Shabbos,* I really had to be determined. They all went while I stayed home alone, but even worse was the look in their eyes which displayed annoyance with my "holier-than-thou" attitude. Now, three years later, there are women in our bungalow colony who occasionally go to a movie. I walk away when I hear them planning these outings. I'm just not tempted to do it anymore.

5. We had always been taught in school about the importance of making *brachos* out loud. I used to wonder why it was such a hard thing to do, though; I'd always chicken out at the last minute. I kept thinking about why people find it so embarrassing to do *"frum"* things in public. Maybe we don't want to seem more righteous than the next person.

   I have a lot of company, mostly singles who come over to chat. I was sitting with the girls around the table one *Shabbos* afternoon, and my brain said, "What is your problem? Why are you so afraid to do a *mitzvah*?" I picked up a glass of juice and quickly mouthed the *brachah* out loud, but only the few people sitting right next to me heard. They glanced up for a brief second and answered *"Amen"* without batting an eyelash. Nobody thought it was weird. I felt much more comfortable doing it afterward, and I felt good about myself too.

6. I taught myself how to do calligraphy and always enjoyed making small plaques or other items as gifts, but I never considered my work very professional. One of my friends works for a company that needed an elaborate piece of calligraphy for a promotional project, and she set up an interview for me, in spite of my protests. I really didn't have much confidence and went only on a lark, but the manager liked my work. I found myself accepting the job and then I heard myself asking for half the money down! To my surprise, the manager agreed.

   I'm not really planning to make a career out of this, but I was amazed at my ability to make a business deal without appearing wishy-washy, especially because I've always been on the shy side. And now I may have some opportunities to make money in the future.

PART III: WRAPPING UP

This section contains an active planner. It is where all the ideas you have been reading about become reality. In it you will find:
1. A review of many of the principles we have discussed.
2. A daily menu for growth.
3. A goal-setting chapter that will help you pack your bags for our ultimate destination.
4. An appendix on public speaking.

Now you can really begin putting your newfound strength to daily use.

Chapter 11

> רַבִּי יַעֲקֹב אוֹמֵר: הָעוֹלָם הַזֶּה דּוֹמֶה לִפְרוֹזְדוֹר בִּפְנֵי הָעוֹלָם הַבָּא, הַתְקֵן עַצְמְךָ בַּפְּרוֹזְדוֹר כְּדֵי שֶׁתִּכָּנֵס לַטְּרַקְלִין.
>
> Rabbi Yaakov said: This world is like a lobby before the World to Come; prepare yourself in the lobby so that you may enter the banquet hall.
>
> (Avos 4:21).

Preparing For The Future

A common game that is played at birthday parties is "I'm Going to Israel and I Will Take Along . . ." Everyone sits in a circle, and each person in turn names something beginning with the given letter of the alphabet that he or she will pack in a suitcase. Each player repeats what everyone else has said and adds something new.

Of course, this is just a child's game, but nostalgia can sometimes provide us with deeper analogies. Does your life have a destination? In order to make each day of our lives worthwhile, we must know what we are doing and why. The goal of this world is to get to *Olam Haba* the World to Come. Rabbi Yaakov says in *Pirkei Avos* (4:21), *"This world is like a lobby before the World to Come; prepare yourself in the lobby so that you may enter the banquet hall."*

When we are about to travel, our preparations are based on the destination. What is the climate like? What will we do there? Who will we be staying with? Can some of the things we need be bought there, or must everything be purchased in advance? It helps to make a list of what we have and what we need.

In *Olam Haba,* the things we will need are very different from those we usually pack in a suitcase. They will not be physical items; instead they will consist of spiritual accomplishments. Our sages emphasize that we must prepare now.

Here is the final exercise in the book. It will help you decide what you want to "take along" with you to *Olam Haba.* You have now reached a stage where you know that growth is possible. Packing this suitcase no longer has to remain a burdensome and unrealistic chore; it can now become a project of joyous anticipation.

1. I'm Going to Olam Haba and I Will Take Along. . .

Write down five items that are already in your spiritual possession. What principles do you firmly uphold? What accomplishments do you have to your credit that you could pack in this imaginary suitcase that you are taking to *Olam Haba?* Your list can include anything from a small act to your struggle to change a trait.

1. _____

2. _____

3. _____

4. _____

5. _____

2. In the Next Five Years:

What will you acquire in the next five years to put in your "suitcase" for *Olam Haba?*

1. _____

2. _____

3. _____

4. _____

5. _____

3. In The Next Year:

What will you pack in your "suitcase" *this* year? These are more specific goals than the ones you had in your last list because they are more immediate. Choose things that are reasonably within your power to accomplish.

1. _____

2. _____

3. _____

4. _____

5. _____

4. Now:

What five things will you do *starting today*? Decide on something simple that you can definitely complete by the end of the week. This is your opportunity to take that first step, even if it is only a small one.

1. _____

2. _____

3. _____

4. _____

5. _____

True Responses

When the idea of establishing goals for the future arose in the workshop, we sat around the table trying to think of things to put in our "suitcases." As had happened so often in the past, many of the women did not think of obvious accomplishments that were right in front of them.

There was Baila, trying to decide what to write. A toddler and an infant were sitting calmly on her lap. They were not pushing or fidgeting, and they looked like they had just come out of the permanent press cycle of the washing machine. "What should I write?" she muttered.

"Your children," someone said. "Look how nicely they behave."

Mirel was just staring at a blank sheet of paper. She really thought she had nothing to write! This was authentic humility. I know Mirel; she is so kind and has done so much.

"Write down the *shidduchim* you have arranged," I suggested.

Someone else offered, "They say that if you have made three *shidduchim*, you enter *Gan Eden* on that merit alone."

When the papers reached my seat, I glanced at them and took a deep breath. The intensity in those responses threw me for a second; it was deeper than it had been in past discussions. The women had opened a window into their hearts and invited me to take a look.

Here is a partial "packing list" from that session, full of heartwarming accomplishments:

I'm Going to Olam Haba and I Will Take Along:

A
1. My persistence in encouraging my child to learn, although he has had great difficulties.
2. My efforts to set up *shidduchim*. So many people that I called were thrilled just to be remembered.
3. Lending a patient ear when others need to talk.
4. The times I have helped to set up others' *simchos*.

B
1. The meals I've cooked for new mothers.
2. The clothing I have sewn for my children.
3. The tears that I cry to Hashem.
4. My effort to improve my relations with others.

C
1. The *mitzvos* my children have done.
2. Kind words that I use to strengthen others.
3. The prayers that I say to Hashem.
4. The pain that is in my heart.

D
1. The happy couples whose matches I arranged.
2. Volunteering at the hospital.
3. My family and all I do for them.
4. Scrap books I have put together from *tzedakah* functions.

E
1. The *tzedakah* I have given.
2. The knowledge I have given to my students.

3. The nights I stayed up with a very sick friend.
4. My involvement with my grandparents.

F

1. The hectic mornings getting my four children off to school. "I always say,'We are going to *Olam Haba* for this, kids.' "
2. My *Shabbos* guests including the ones who are not that easy to invite.
3. The retarded children I work with and their parents.
4. The many rides I've given to friends who could not drive or did not have a car at their disposal.

Chapter 12

> בֶּן עַזַּאי אוֹמֵר: הֱוֵי רָץ לְמִצְוָה קַלָּה, וּבוֹרֵחַ מִן הָעֲבֵרָה; שֶׁמִּצְוָה גּוֹרֶרֶת מִצְוָה, וַעֲבֵרָה גוֹרֶרֶת עֲבֵרָה, שֶׁשְּׂכַר מִצְוָה מִצְוָה, וּשְׂכַר עֲבֵרָה עֲבֵרָה.
>
> Ben Azzai said: Run to perform even a 'minor' mitzvah, and flee from sin; for one mitzvah leads to another mitzvah, and one sin leads to another sin; for the consequence of a mitzvah is a mitzvah, and the consequence of a sin is a sin.
>
> (Avos 4:2)

The Daily Menu

It feels good to plan. Planning reminds us that we are on earth for a purpose, and gives us the feeling of being on a treasure hunt. Yet the danger is that we will put the plan away after a week and not do anything with it.

The key, as we've discussed before, is to do something right now no matter how small. If you decide to do something simple right now, it will help you to feel good about yourself. Learning is a process that happens very gradually. When you can point to even a simple success, you can generate the positive feedback you need to persist, and you will wind up doing more than you expected to do.

In order to foster your "stick-to-it-iveness," I am providing you with a daily menu of options for growth, which incorporate the ideas we have discussed in the book. You don't have to do them all at once. Pick one or two but do something!

1. Wake Up With Joy.

The Rebbe of Vorke quotes this verse in *Tehillim* (90:14): שַׂבְּעֵנוּ בַבֹּקֶר חַסְדֶּךָ וּנְרַנְּנָה וְנִשְׂמְחָה בְּכָל יָמֵינוּ, *Satisfy us in the morning with Your kindness, then we shall sing out and rejoice throught our days.*

We learn from this that if our mornings are filled with an awareness of the kindness of Hashem, we will be joyful the entire day. Awareness includes appreciation of the "little things" in life, just as we discussed in the very first chapter of the book.

> *The routine of the day begins with saying "Modeh Ani" — I thank You, Hashem. This is said even before the morning washing of the hands, while one's hands are "impure." The reason is that all the impurities of the world do not defile a Jew's Modeh Ani. He might be lacking in perfection in one thing or another, but his gratitude to G-d remains intact.*
>
> (*Hayom Yom*, by Rabbi Yosef Yitchok Shneerson).

One of my friends says, "It's a beautiful morning," so often that her children have caught on. "It's not enough just to notice the good," she says. "You have to *embellish* the good. Enjoy every flower and every tree and every bird and thank Hashem."

2. Perform One Small Act.

Choose a small act that you know you can repeat successfully.

In *Pirkei Avos* (3:19) Rabbi Akiva says, "וְהַכֹּל לְפִי רוֹב הַמַּעֲשֶׂה, Everything is relative to **how many times** you do a good deed." With this verse, the Rambam explains that one who gives a single dollar one hundred times to one hundred poor people is superior to one who gives one hundred dollars once.

Small acts that are repeated help us change and grow. Through giving charity repeatedly, we become kinder people. We internalize the belief that all the money and possessions we have are a gift from Hashem.

Another benefit is that each mitzvah adds up. Rabbi Ezriel Tauber explains in *Choose Life* that with each moment of life, we double, triple, and quadruple the level of closeness to Hashem that we have thus far attained.

And we all know the famous advice our parents have given us about "saving pennies."

3. Encourage Others

> *"When I was young, I learned that it was a great accomplishment to write an original Torah thought. Now I see that it is a great accomplishment to make an elderly widow happy."* (Rav Chaim Ozer Grodzensky in a conversation with Rabbi Mendel Zaks)

Rabbi Avigdor Miller explains that one of Hashem's special acts of kindness is that He encourages the humble. We should try to perform such a kindness at least once every day. You know how you feel when someone gives you a compliment or an encouraging word. You also know that you make a conscious effort to strengthen your relationship with a person who shows you warmth and approval. It doesn't cost much to smile and say something pleasant, but the profits are endless.

Mrs. D. told me that she once noticed a mother who came to a lecture accompanied by her twin daughters, who must have been about eighteen years old. The daughters sat on either side of their mother, and all three were really enjoying the lecture. "I was so impressed," said Mrs. D., "that I called the mother that Friday to compliment her. I told her that I just wanted her to know that I thought she was very fortunate to have such wonderful daughters who agree to attend Torah lectures with their mother, and I wished her a lot of *nachas*."

" 'Is there any other reason for your call?' the mother asked.

" 'No, I just wanted to compliment you on your daughters,' replied Mrs. D.

"This mother was so enthusiastically appreciative that I called her. I saw that everyone needs a good word now and then," Mrs. D. remarked.

4. Decide to Forgive One Insult Every Day.

Raizy was relaxing on the terrace with her husband when a sudden downpour of water hit them squarely, soaking Raizy's *sheitel* and her husband's head and shirt. "What is this?" they yelled up to the second-floor window.

The neighbor replied, "I didn't know you were sitting there," and then retreated.

Later that day they faced the woman on the steps, hoping for an apology. Instead the neighbor said, "You never sit in that corner. Why did you pick that corner just today?"

Raizy didn't answer. Her husband asked her afterward why she kept quiet. She replied, "If I would have screamed and given her a piece of my mind, what would I have gained from it?"

Speaking up when there is nothing to be gained provokes quarrels and needlessly prolongs our own distress. If we forget about it and go on with life, we will have fewer ulcers. There are many important things we must speak up about, but each of us can find one triviality a day that can be absorbed. Give the benefit of the doubt.

5. Learn a Little Bit On the Phone With a Friend Each Day

At 9:15 every morning instead of diving into the housework, I go to the phone and call my friend Goldie. We both reach for our copies of *Gateway to Happiness* by Rabbi Zelig Pliskin. For five minutes a day for six months now, we have taken turns reading a paragraph or two and sharing our feelings.

When we finish a paragraph, one of us usually comments, "Wow!" Then there is a quiet pause, and the other invariably says, "That reminds me of something that happened last week..."

We could each learn on our own, but it wouldn't be the same. The words of the *sefer* have a deeper meaning when they are shared, and are remembered longer. The partnership also provides a stronger impetus for taking action. Sharing our experiences each day makes the crucial difference between wishful dreaming and actual *doing*.

A third benefit is the wonderful friendship that can develop. Goldie and I have become so much closer through our daily contact in Torah learning. Whenever I feel overwhelmed, I know I can talk things over with her.

When Rabbi Ezriel Tauber reviewed the original manuscript, he suggested that husband and wife learn together each day. He said, "this is the best way to increase healthy communication."

6. Have Your Sefarim and Torah Tapes On Hand and Ready For Use

Yesterday you attended an inspiring lecture on *Sh'miras Halashon* and decided to review the pertinent laws. Now you have ten free minutes, but where on earth is that copy of *Guard Your Tongue* that you received as a graduation present?

The most common complaint I hear from mothers is that they intended to learn but were delayed because they could not find the *sefer* they needed. Our time is so limited that if we have to spend time searching for something, there won't be time left to use it. If the *sefer* is there when you have a spare moment, you will pick it up and look inside. If you have to go and get it, you will put it off and forget about it. Those little bits and snatches of learning are lost opportunities.

It is not only useful to have the *sefarim* we learn from on hand. It feels good. Seeing the *siddur* or *sefer* on the kitchen shelf as I pass it while doing other things reminds me of my goals.

The last *mitzvah* of the Torah is to write a *Sefer Torah*. The *Sefer HaChinuch* explains, "It is known that people accomplish according to their preparation and what they have conveniently at hand. Therefore, Hashem commanded each person to have a written *Sefer Torah* in his home so that he can learn from it at all times and will not need to go to his friend . . . Each individual is bound by this commandment . . . Although the obligation in the Torah applies mainly to a *Sefer Torah*, there is no doubt that any book based on Torah is included in this precept. When one has beautiful new *sefarim*, he learns with greater joy. The way of those who fear Hashem is to have a special room for their *sefarim* and to acquire many *sefarim* according to their means."

There are so many moments that are ideal for listening to Torah tapes. However, you will miss them if you aren't prepared. My husband bought me a wonderful gift: a set of rechargeable batteries and a charger. Now I no longer run out of batteries. I listen to Torah tapes when I ride in a car service or before I fall asleep at night; it helps me sleep better.

Do you have a *siddur* on hand in your kitchen? Do you carry one with you in your pocketbook? Make what you need available now.

7. Write Down Five Things You Have Done Right Each Day and Thank Hashem For the Success.

> *The smallest victory that you win (over the Yetzer Hara), the slightest increase in your power over him, regard as important so that it may be a step to greater victory.* (Duties of The Heart)

Cleaning an extra drawer for *Pesach* may not be your idea of a high old time, but it is surprising how quickly you can come to like the chore when you know you can triumphantly mark it down as one of the five things you did right today.

The principal idea to remember about the time spent on spiritual growth is that if you start to see it as drudgery, you will soon give it up in defeat. After all, it ought to be a pleasure to serve Hashem. If you rearrange your mental pattern so that your spiritual goals coincide with your routine tasks, before you know it you will have fifty *mitzvos* on your list that you were not doing regularly before.

Chapter 13

> הַשְׁלֵךְ עַל ה', יְהָבְךָ וְהוּא יְכַלְכְּלֶךָ
> Cast your cares upon G-d, and He will support you.
>
> (*Tehillim* 55:23)

The Last Word

Can this really be the end? I feel like I have just had a lovely visit with a good friend. You are about to leave, but while the door is still open and we are both standing, I cannot resist having one last word.

> A child stands on the dining room chair. He leans on the windowsill and looks out, pressing his nose to the misty window. He is thinking about the snow, imagining that it tastes like vanilla ice cream. He wants to go

out but he is afraid; the snow outside is very deep, and he might slip and fall.

He runs to get his new red rubber boots and mittens and brings them to his father. His father smiles and agrees to take him out. "We will go together," he assures him. "I will hold your hand."

They walk outside together. The little boy holds his father's hand tightly. He trusts his father and knows he won't fall now. If we truly understand that Hashem is holding our hand, the obstacles are no longer overwhelming. (told by Harav Nadav *Shlita*)

Most of the challenges we have tried to tackle in this book can be traced to one basic problem: a lack of self-esteem. If we think carefully for a moment about this very simple story of the boy and his father, we might see that underlying the basic principle of faith in G-d is an even more fundamental concept.

Someone once told me that G-d does not create faulty products. Everything He made is exactly as He wanted it, and each creation is beloved by Him. That includes you.

The poor self-image that we nurture so fiercely is a fabrication of our minds. G-d thinks much better of us than we think of ourselves. He cherishes us and would never leave us out in the cold.

Stories about children often convey this idea poignantly, because the innocent faith of a child is a phenomenon that can reach anyone's heart. But we have forgotten that we are all the children of Hashem, capable of entrusting ourselves to His care with the same whole and simple faith of the child who holds his father's hand in the snow.

Here is the last "true response" in the book. I think it will touch you as deeply as it touched me. Chaia Erblich, whom we have met before, told me this story:

"I found myself at a weekend seminar. To my amazement, I found that some of the lectures were beginning to have an effect on me. On the third night, as I was lying in bed, I suddenly started to utter *Krias Shema*. It had been a long time since I had said the night prayer with any degree of awareness or concentration. Tears were trickling down my cheeks. The words I was whispering sounded sweeter than any lullaby I had ever heard.

"No, actually that wasn't true. I began to remember. Once oh, so long ago when I was little, perhaps five or six, *Krias Shema* had brought me this same sweet feeling, had wiped away my fear and apprehension. I knew now: It had been on *Pesach* night, when I was about to go to sleep. I remembered my father coming over to cover me.

" 'Why are you smiling, Chaia?' " he asked.

" 'I am smiling because tonight I don't have to say *Shema*. Because tonight Hashem watches over all His children. They don't even have to ask for it.'

"My faith was so complete and real. How could I ever have forgotten those happy days? And as I was thinking about the past, it suddenly dawned on me, not since I was a little girl had I truly felt happy and carefree. Only then, far back in the past, had I really known peace.

"I drew out my prayer now, trying to make each word last. When I finished, I added a silent plea: 'Please, Hashem, please don't let me forget. Don't let me take the wonderful taste of *Krias Shema* for granted. Allow me to feel every night, forever, like I felt when I was five years old.' "

This is the best thing that we can wish for, and it is possible. If we want a clear awareness that Hashem is guarding us as His children, all we have to do is make Him our Father.

Hashem wants the best for us, just as every parent wants his child to succeed, and He will be there to help us, no matter what happens. He knows we can do the things we dream of; He knows our abilities better than we do.

In fact, He is the One who has told each of us, "There will never be another you."

Appendix: Confidence In Public Speaking

Gila was asked to speak in Williamsburg for a twelfth-grade class, and she called me in desperation. "When is your book coming out?" she asked. "I need to read it now. I'm nervous I have to go talk for this class in an hour! I don't like to talk to a group. What if I sound repetitive? What if I can't find the right words? What if they ask a question I can't answer? You must know what to do if you wrote this book and you give so many lectures."

Shaindy promised to give a Friday night lecture at someone's home on her block, and even though the women are people she knows, she feels very uncomfortable.

Penina wants to start a regular group to learn *Navi* in her home, but she cannot find a teacher and is afraid she will lack sufficient committed participants to assure the teacher's payment.

Chaya Sara is treasurer of the G.O. in her school and was asked to give a *Dvar Torah* at the next school assembly.

These are a few of the many people who dream of giving lectures one day, or need to speak right now and do not know how to start. If you are among them, it will encourage you to know that if you have some basic aptitude, speaking is a skill that can be learned. The secret is practice. Everyone was once a beginner at something they do well today. I now give at least three lectures or workshops a week; at times I have spoken for crowds of a thousand women, but I am sure that my lectures were not as good when I first started as they are now. Practice builds confidence and helps one do a better job. However (and you should know this if you have read the rest of this book), you should not be afraid to start!

Why Speak?

There are many good reasons to consider giving lectures. Do not do it if you think it is easy and will earn you a lot of money. Preparing a lecture is a great deal of work, and the financial returns are negligible. Frequently, you will speak as a volunteer, and if you do get paid, the money will probably just cover your expenses. But there are other more valuable returns.

You may want to speak because you really care about a particular subject and would like to share it with others. Or you may be home with a baby or two and would like to have some group involvement, but you don't want to leave the children to take a regular teaching job. Or you may really need this skill right now in order to advance your career or to give an award at the next luncheon.

How do you know if you have the potential? Many people have a natural flair for communication, and they will probably deny it when you try to compliment them. One of my friends always has an eager audience because she tells stories in such a colorful way. When I mentioned to her that she ought to take a turn heading the workshop, she shrugged and said, "I'm just good at simple conversation." Being "good at simple conversation" is a pretty solid credential, certainly enough to get you started. If you have that talent, you could be using it for a higher purpose.

Do you have a ready smile? Do you believe that people are basically good? Are you sensitive to their emotions? Do you notice problems that need to be tackled? Do you have strong convictions? Can you share knowledge without making others feel stupid? Do people feel good around you? Are you interested in learning from others?

If you can answer yes to these questions, you are ready to start a step-by-step plan for preparing a speech.

The Topic

The first two basic questions you will have to answer are: What is the projected length, and what is the topic? You should be able to describe your topic in three sentences before you start your research. It is not enough to decide that you want to speak about antidotes to stress. You need to be more specific.

When I was a student teacher in Jerusalem, I once spent *Shabbos* at the home of Rabbi Jaffe, one of my teachers. I told him that I would be giving a model lesson about *Ahavas Torah*. He looked at me and asked, "What will you say?"

I replied, "Well, I don't know yet. I guess I'll look in a lot of different books, and when I see a nice idea I'll write it down, and when I have enough for a lesson I'll stop."

Rabbi Jaffe looked solemn. "If you work on it that way, it can take months, and the lesson still won't be clear. First tell me four things you really want to say about the topic. Then, if I have a source to suggest, I'll give it to you now."

After a few minutes of silent thought I said, "I guess what I really want to say is that knowing facts isn't worth much if you don't honestly fear Hashem and love Torah. I also want to encourage the girls and tell them that they can acquire a love of the Torah it's necessary and within reach."

Rabbi Jaffe smiled, letting me know that I was on the right track. "You might want to look up some people from *Tanach* who were learned and yet rebelled against Torah, such as Doeg and Achitophel. I also have a *sefer* you can use, so come back during the week."

When I came back on Sunday evening, Rabbi Jaffe explained, "The *sefer* I am giving you is out of print. It contains the *mussar* lectures of my *rebbe*, Rav Chezkel Levenstein, *zt"l*. I love this *sefer* very much, but I will trust you with it. Please be sure to return it by Tuesday evening."

My mumbled thanks did not express my deep feelings. I was both impressed and encouraged by Rabbi Jaffe's trust. He had shown confidence in me and made me feel that I wasn't a child anymore. He had also given me a crucial piece of concrete advice: Be specific.

Organizing the Lecture

Now that you have narrowed down your topic, you are ready to begin preparing your lecture. Rebbetzin Yehudis Grunfeld, *tichye*, who is still speaking at eighty-plus and is one of the most dramatic and eloquent people I have ever met, once said, "A good lecture has a good beginning, a good ending, and not too much in the middle."

The title of a lecture and its introduction should tell people immediately what to expect. The introduction may consist of a list of questions you will answer, or it may be a story or parable that sets the theme. You must set the mood in the first five minutes and communicate to the audience that they can expect something good. The opening of the lecture should always generate the same type of pleasant exhilaration you have when you walk into a room where a beautiful buffet is laid out. The delicious aroma of the food is tantalizing and arouses positive expectations.

The central portion of the lecture needs balance. You need a main course, and you need something to augment it and add color. Sometimes a lecture has no meat at all. It's full of anecdotes but nothing strong is said. People dislike it when you don't trust them enough to give them substantial material; it makes them feel inferior. On the other hand, a lecture that is all facts and no spice can be tedious. It is hard to build up an appetite on a dinner of boiled chicken. You need to find the happy medium.

To amplify the facts and make them interesting, you must use examples to support your ideas particularly examples that involve people. Stories and incidents help the audience to digest the main point. You can find such examples by looking in the indices of several biographies or by looking in *sefarim* which have personalities arranged alphabetically. (*Pele Yo'eitz* and *Ishei Tanach* are two good sources.) Your best resource, however, is your own knowledge and experience. The best ideas are saved up in your brain. Prayer also helps! When I can't think of a good way to explain something, I close my eyes and say, "*Lishuas'cha kivisi Hashem,*" and Hashem sends me wonderful ideas. Sometimes I say, "*Lishuas'cha kivisi Hashem,*" and open a *sefer* at random, and there is the story I need, right on the page in front of me. I have found excellent material that way.

If you insert *mussar,* use it only to pepper your speech. It can add flavor, but too much of even the best message becomes impossible to digest. My rule is: Do not advise others to do what you would not do yourself.

Finally, you need a conclusion. The conclusion should leave a sweet taste. It could be a personal story, a moving poem, a hopeful *midrash,* or a story about a *tzaddik.* I've found material for some of my conclusions in *The Jewish Observer, Good Fortune,* Torah biographies, and various cassette tapes. If possible, I give the participants a printed copy of the story or poem I used to take home.

Confidence

You are probably smiling as you read this and thinking, "Hmm, do you really think my only problem is knowing what to say? I'm scared stiff to stand up in front of an audience! I just know that I'll forget everything I've prepared, and stutter, and make mistakes, and feel like a fool."

What I'm going to tell you now is critical for every speaker to know: It is okay and even preferable to be human!

Recently at a charity dinner that I attended, huge screens were set up near the tables so that everyone in the ballroom could see the speakers clearly. All of the speakers that evening read from papers in front of them. They thought they were creating the illusion of addressing the audience directly by looking up at us after every three words. Up and down, up and down went the speakers' heads until I felt dizzy, and I left the dinner with a headache. Why were they so dependent on that paper in front of them? Why were they afraid of using one or two wrong words? Did they really think I would remember each syllable they uttered?

I remember my first lecture. I was a junior in high school. We had gone to an international Bais Yaakov convention, and we were responsible to deliver a synopsis of all the Torah discourses that we had heard. Someone volunteered my services without my knowledge: "I think Roiza should do it. She is the only one who was listening to all the speeches." Our assistant principal, Rebbetzin Malka Paretsky, gave me two pointers that were the foundation of my speaking career:

"The audience needs to feel that you are talking to them. They want to see you and feel with you. Their attention is not totally focused on the words you use. They care about *you*.

"Make sure, too, that every point you present is clear. You might think that if half your message is strong, it will somehow camouflage the parts that are not well thought-out. This will not work, because any item that is puzzling distracts our attention and causes us to miss completely what the speaker says subsequently."

I did not really believe her. Could it be that the words themselves were not the most important part of the speech? Now, after having ten years of practice in both speaking and listening, I see that she is right. The audience wants *you*.

A well-known lecturer in our area once said, "I do not speak because I'm a speaker, but because I have something to say." This man's accent is noticeable, and his sentences are fragmented; yet everyone runs to hear him speak. His strength is in understanding people. He doesn't speak from an ivory tower. He perceives what people cry about, worry about, wonder about, and struggle with. His lectures answer the questions people labor to express. He knows what will give them hope, and he's not afraid to share his own life.

Understanding both the value of your own personality and the value of your message will help you overcome the fear of forgetting. By the same token, a single-minded focus on the individual words in the speech can lead to the very disaster you want to avoid. The only time I ever went blank was during a speech at my high school graduation. Every word of my address was approved by a member of the staff who had told me in very serious tones that I was representing the entire school with my every syllable. In the middle of my address I suddenly forgot the next word and then everything else in the address. I thought I would fall through the platform, but Hashem was with me! The next word I needed was in the top sentence on the page I looked at.

Do not think of the words. Think instead of the concepts you will be relating, and you will do fine. There is one exception to this rule, and that is when you quote others. Here you must not rely on your memory; either copy the quotation carefully or bring along the original source. This is important not only in order to give due credit to the person whose words you are using, but also to maintain your own credibility. There is bound to be someone in the audience who will catch the misquotation and think, "Hmm, what a silly error. Even I know that."

If you realize, however, that you *have* made a mistake during your speech, admit it and the audience will forgive you. One summer when I spoke for Bais Yaakov, I suddenly forgot a part of the prayer that I intended to quote. I turned to five hundred people and said, "I'm sorry I forgot the end of this *pasuk*. Can someone finish it for me?" Everyone laughed, and I continued the lecture.

Perhaps you think you just could not say something like that in front of five hundred people. Don't worry. It takes time before you can trust an audience and let your own personality shine through. This sense of trust comes from the audience itself, when it is clear that they have really bonded to you. I know I have succeeded when I feel an aura in the room as I say the last sentence, a certain silence in the air that tells me my words have been heard. Sometimes people leave quickly because they do not want me to see that their eyes are watery; others come up to ask me a question, to say thank you, or to share their own experiences.

In that very first lecture that I gave as a junior in high school, I spoke about the importance of praying sincerely for others. I concluded with this thought: "When I was in ninth grade, my grandmother fell into a coma. Until that time, whenever I had prayed for the sick people on the *Tehillim* list, I had thought of the list as a bunch of names. But when I wrote my grandmother's name on the list, it was not just a name. I wrote it with tears in my eyes, hoping that everyone would remember to pray for her. She was *my* grandmother. Please remember that every name on the list is someone's father, mother, grandmother, grandfather, son, or daughter."

When I came down from the podium, I was surrounded by my classmates. I remember one friend whose look was piercing. "When my father was sick, I also asked people to pray for him," she said to me. "When he recovered, I felt like I wanted to hug every person in the class. Roiza, thank you for telling everyone, because that is exactly the way it is."

Yael's words lifted me up so high that I thought I could touch the sky. דְּבָרִים הַיּוֹצְאִים מִן הַלֵּב נִכְנָסִים אֶל הַלֵּב "When you speak, you carve a window into your heart and allow the audience to see what you really feel. If you know that they have understood, there is a meeting of hearts" (*Sefer Shiras Yisrael,* R' Moshe Ibn Ezra).

Baruch Hashem, I have filled my life with that indescribable joy, and I hope you will too.

Index

actions   111, 112-118
advice (afraid to ask)   67
afraid of people   100
anger   42
anxiety   98
anxious   94
appreciation for / what we have / ourselves   28
assumptions   42
avoid change   60
awesome war   73
Baal Shem Tov   60
be yourself   29
beginning   117
behavior patterns   69
benefit of the doubt   46
benefits   61
Bitachon   96--100
bound to Above   97
breathing   26
change   60, 61, 70
Chanukah   116
cheerful   24
chest of gems   101
Chovos HaLevavos   65, 69
closeness to Hashem   136
cobweb   67
common dreams   63
communication   138
comparing   31
comparing goals   63
confidence   45, 145
conflict   60
cope   *Introduction*
coping skills   *Introduction*
correcting wrong   78
daily routine   134
depend on Hashem   96-100

despair   75
determination   *Introduction,* 97
developing friendships   49-53, 137
difficulties with people   44
discouraged / discouraging thoughts   75, 77
dissolving panic   96
don't give up   70
doubts   71
each moment of life   136
effort (earnestly try)   *Introduction,* 80
emotional atmosphere   89
encourage others   136
exercises / doing them   22
exercise — gratitude / five things done right   32
expectations   149
failure (temporary)   75, 77
feel like a flop   77
five things done right   32-36
five minutes   134
focus on the positive (on the good)   *Introduction,* 32
gam zu l'tovah   90
goals   63
good deeds   73
good thing right now   87
gratitude   22, 26
gratitude exercise   26
great men   73
guilt   77
handicaps   24
happiness / dependent on thoughts   21
heart follows deed   112-118
heavenly voice   60
how do you feel (exercise)   61

Index □ 155

hurdles   74
impossible dream   104, 105
inner resources   103
knowledge   53
last-minute fears   95
limitations   79
lion-skin jacket (Dovid HaMelech)   104
measuring   30
Menorah   116
mission in life   30
Modeh Ani   135
mothers-in-law   33
motivation (self-motivation)   116, 118
never disappointed   25
never too late   70
no mitzvah is small   133, 139
notice the good   135
now   129
obstacles, falls and slumps   55, 73
Olam Haba (exercise)   126
opportunities   58
panic / un-panic   94, 97
permanent changes   *Introduction*
planning   126
positive person   87
potential   106
power to improve   70
pressure   22
problems   25
procrastinate   116

Rabbi Akiva   70
Rabbeinu Bachya   22, 64
renew positive experiences   102, 104
reward for effort   80
sadness (recovering from)   87
satisfaction in life   21
security   71
see good in oneself   28
setback   73
sharing experiences   63
shidduch   90
simchah   *Introduction*
simple success   87
sleep better   114
small acts   133, 134
speak softly   89
staying calm   42
success   106
support and praise   46
telephone Torah learning   137
tension   44
teshuvah   78
this week's goals   112
tired   25, 89
today   32-34, 113
tomorrow syndrome   115
Torah study   137
triumph   104, 106
true servant of Hashem   31
true success   87
trying new things   59

About the Author

Roiza Devora Weinreich has designed and presented practical workshops based on Torah principles and true success stories for the past seven years. Among the organizations she has spoken for are Ohr Somayach Alumni, Shalheves, Bais Yaakov Alumni, The Jewish Renaissance Center and Bnos Zion of Bobov. Some topics now on cassette tape are: "How To Find More Time and Energy," "Eight Things You Can Do for Your Children," and "Antidotes To Stress". If you are interested in more information or if you would like to order the weekly newsletter or the lectures on cassette tape, send a self-addressed envelope to: Roiza Weinreich, 625 Avenue L, Brooklyn, NY 11230.

This volume is part of
THE ARTSCROLL SERIES®
an ongoing project of
translations, commentaries and expositions
on Scripture, Mishnah, Talmud, Halachah,
liturgy, histroy, the classic Rabbinic writings,
biographies, and thought.

For a brochure of current publications
visit your local Hebrew bookseller
or contact the publisher:

Mesorah Publications, ltd

4401 Second Avenue
Brooklyn, New York 11232
(718) 921-9000